COLLECTOR'S GUIDE TO
DOLLS
of the
1960S and 1970S
VOLUME II
IDENTIFICATION AND VALUES

CINDY SABULIS

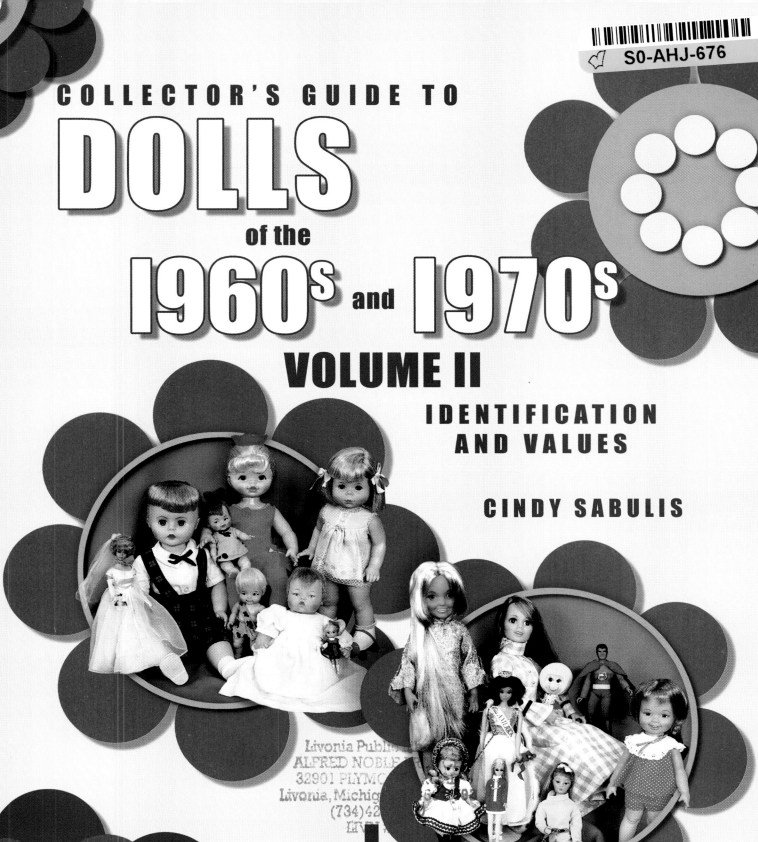

COLLECTOR BOOKS

A Division of Schroeder Publishing Co., Inc.

On the cover:

1960s dolls, front row: 8" Ideal Bamm-Bamm, 14" Ideal Tiny Thumbelina, Hasbro Go-Team-Go Dolly Darling. Back row: Mattel Bubblecut Barbie, Deluxe Reading Suzy Smart, 8" Ideal Pebbles, Mattel Dancerina, Mattel Baby First Step.
1970s dolls, front row: Madame Alexander Hungarian, Topper Toys Fancy Feet, Uneeda Dollikin, Ideal Cinnamon. Center: Mattel Walk Lively Miss America. Back row: Ideal Brandi, Ideal Harmony, Mattel Talkup, Mego Superman.

Catalog pages reprinted in this book are courtesy of the following companies:
Sears, Roebuck and Co. Archives, Hoffman Estates, Illinois
J.C. Penneys
Montgomery Ward and Co.

Any corrections to information printed within this book or contribution of photos for future use can be sent to the author c/o Toys of Another Time, L.L.C., P.O. Box 642, Shelton, CT 06484. Submissions are gratefully appreciated, however, no letters or photos can be acknowledged or returned.

Cover design by Beth Summers
Book design by Holly C. Long
Photographs without credits by Cindy Sabulis

3 9082 09669 0030

Collector Books
P. O. Box 3009
Paducah, KY 42002-3009

www.collectorbooks.com

Copyright © 2004 Cindy Sabulis

The current values in this book should be used only as a guide. They are not intended to set prices, which vary from one section of the country to another. Auction prices as well as dealer prices vary greatly and are affected by condition as well as demand. Neither the author nor the publisher assumes responsibility for any losses that might be incurred as a result of consulting this guide.

Searching For A Publisher?

We are always looking for knowledgeable people considered to be experts within their fields. If you feel that there is a real need for a book on your collectible subject and have a large comprehensive collection, contact Collector Books.

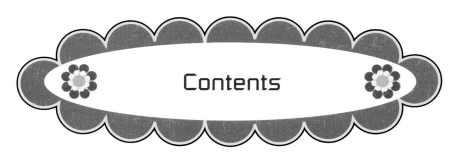

Contents

Dedication

Dolls have been a part of my life for as long as I can remember. I went right from playing with them to collecting them. Dolls are, and have always been, important to me, but compared to children they are nothing. If I had to choose between a million dolls and one child, I'd choose the child. This book is dedicated to the most important child in my life, my son David.

Acknowledgments

Compiling a reference book such as this one is difficult to do alone. It was only with the help of many collectors willing to share information and photos of their dolls that I was able to complete this book. I am indebted to the following contributors who allowed me to photograph their dolls or who took the time to take photographs of their dolls for me, and/or generously shared information with me that I needed for this book:

Carole Lacy Bailey
Jennie Brott
Michele Casino
Sharon Criscione
Karen Edland
Robin Englehart from Vintagelane.com
Karen Hickey
Hillary and Cliff James from Toy with Me
Janet and Mike Lawrence
Dal Lowenbein
Joyce McCandless
Elaine McGrath

Nancy Jean Mong
Lisa Petrucci
Nancy Ruppenthal
Mark Salyers
Sally Seikel
Rebecca Sevrin
Gloria Telep
Dawn Thomas
Kathleen Tornikoski from Romancing the Doll
Ann Wagner
Sharon Wendrow from Memory Lane
Rebecca Wingler

Special thanks go to Robin Englehart of Vintagelane.com for her never-ending generosity in sharing photos of her dolls. Without her help, a great many of the dolls in this book would not have been included. Thanks go to my brother-in-law, John Sabulis, and my friend, Dal Lowenbein, for the use of their cameras after mine died mid-way through this project. Thanks also to all the fun-loving and big-hearted Kiddle Kollectors in the Klubhouse and the wonderfully generous Tammy collectors I have met through the yearly Tammy convention. The continual praise from these two groups of collectors and the positive comments they have made about my books have reinforced the reasons I continue to write them. Also, thanks go to my good friend, Dal Lowenbein, whose enthusiasm for dolls and life in general helped keep my spirits up when my work load seemed overwhelming. And thanks go to my husband, Steve, who at times had to take over both the doll business and all the household chores so that I could work on this book.

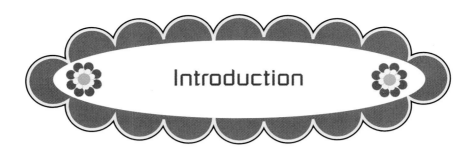

Introduction

After completing my previous book, *Dolls of the 1960s and 1970s,* I felt there were so many more dolls from that period that hadn't made it into the book. So, with the intent to fill some of the gap left from the first book, I began compiling this one. The dolls I selected to show in this volume include dolls that many of our customers from our doll business have requested over the past few years or that collectors seem to be gravitating toward. I have also tried to include a number of dolls that collectors may have seen in their travels, but not known what they were. Some dolls that made their appearance in the first volume of *Dolls of the 1960s and 1970s* appear in this volume as well, many of them now shown mint-in-box or in different variations. At the request of many collectors who I've spoken with, I also included a few fashions for some of the dolls in this book. Although not a complete fashion reference guide for these dolls, the photos will offer some assistance in identifying loose doll clothing.

 ## Using this Guide

Most of the dolls in this book are listed under their manufacturer with the manufacturers listed alphabetically. The dolls are not always listed chronologically, for the sake of keeping all the dolls in a particular line or category together. Whenever possible, dolls are shown wearing their original outfit. If the outfit the doll is pictured in is known not to be original to the doll, it will say so in the text.

 ## Doll Markings

When available, markings for dolls are included as an additional means of helping the reader identify their particular doll. While not much fun to read, it does offer some aid if the reader is unsure of the doll they have. When a slash (/) is present in the listed markings, it indicates a new line of the doll's marking so, "1970/IDEAL TOY CORP./E9-2-H165/HONG KONG" actually would appear on the doll as:

1970
IDEAL TOY CORP.
E9-2-H165
HONG KONG

In most cases, the markings included in the text are the markings on the doll(s) pictured in the photograph, but it's not uncommon for several examples of the same doll to be marked slightly different from each other. Markings on dolls can vary depending on the version or issue date of the doll, the mold used, or the doll's factory origin.

 ## Size of Dolls

The sizes of the dolls shown in the photographs are usually noted in the text. However, the manufacturing process of a doll can sometimes result in the same doll coming out in slightly varying sizes. Depending on how dolls are measured, results can be slightly different as well. For these reasons, there is often a discrepancy from one source to the next on how large or small a doll is. There is really no right or wrong way to measure a doll. Some people measure a doll from the tip of the head to the tip of the toes. Others measure from head to heel. If the doll has a pointed toe, this can result in different measurements. If the doll has a bent leg such as with a baby doll, one can measure all the way along the bent leg with a tape measure or one can straighten out the leg as best as possible and then measure. Either way, there will be a slightly different height assessment. Even something as minor as how far down a doll's head is pushed on her neck can result in different measurements of the same doll. With this in mind, understand that when size is given, it might vary slightly from the size you get when you measure your doll.

Today's Market

Since the first volume of *Dolls of the 1960s and 1970s* was published, the collecting world has seen a drastic change in the buying and selling of collectibles in large part due to the excessive use of the Internet. Many collectibles, including dolls from the 1960s and 1970s, have come out of attics and basements at a faster rate than ever before as more people join the ranks of sellers through online auctions. The supply of vintage dolls for sale has increased, creating a buyers' market for collectors. Some items that used to be considered rare now can be found easily by searching the Internet. Not only can buyers find one example of a doll they've been looking for, they can find a great many of them and so can pick and choose which one they want to buy. While vintage dolls have fared better than many of the newer "limited edition" collectibles in keeping their value, there are many vintage dolls that have come down in value because of this increase in supply. Dolls that were originally produced in large numbers are one group of dolls that have fallen in price since so many of them have survived and are now making it to the resale market. Dolls in played with condition are another group of dolls that has fallen in value. Collectors can wait and easily locate better examples of the same dolls in a short period of time. Unless priced reasonably, dolls in played with condition (i.e. messed up or thinning hair, undressed, stained vinyl, broken fingers, etc.) are passed by more often then they used to be. Of course, not all dolls have gone down in value. Some have gone up because of increased interest in them due in part to the exposure they have received either via the Internet or some other medium. Mint examples of dolls, mint-in-box (MIB) dolls, or never removed from box (NRFB) dolls are still commanding top dollar. Many dolls that are still considered rare or hard to find often have enough collectors interested in them that online auction prices for them have remained extremely competitive and their selling prices continue to climb.

Time to Sell

Many collectors reach the point where they need to weed out their collections either due to space or money constraints, or simply because they decide they don't like a doll. Deciding when to sell can make the difference between getting top dollar for the doll, selling it at cost, or selling it for less then what was originally paid for it. The doll market has become like the stock market with highs and lows changing regularly based on such things as the economy, the season of the year, and even the weather. When it comes time to sell, these factors need to be taken into consideration. Are people spending money on "luxury" items at the moment? If the unemployment rate is high, few people will have the money they need to purchase collectibles, including dolls. Selling prices now seem to be affected by the season of the year as well. Online auctions appear to be more competitive and ending prices higher in the cold weather when more people are home on their computers. A snow storm in different parts of the country could mean more people inside shopping for dolls from their computers. The same holds true for a rainy weekend. Around the holidays a large number of people purchase dolls for gifts or to treat themselves with money they received as a gift. It used to be my belief that people wouldn't buy dolls around the holidays due to cash shortage, and yet, sales for many doll dealers are higher in November and early December than at other times of the year. As a seller you need to take into consideration these things. At different times of the year, you may need to settle for a lower price for a doll then you would at other times. Timing the sale of a doll to when the selling market is high would be nice, of course, but is not always possible.

Determining Value

Online auctions, most notably eBay, have made the task of determining values of collectibles much harder now than it used to be. One day a doll may sell for an outrageous sum of money on eBay only to have another example of it sell for a much lower amount the next week. Some people see either the high ending price or the low ending price of an online auction for a doll similar to theirs and they might think their doll is worth the same amount they saw it sell for. Unfortunately, eBay doesn't always offer a realistic indication of what a doll is worth. I have seen many dolls within the pages of this book sell for a low price on eBay and sell much higher through a dealer, or vice versa. My task was to take those unrealistic high or low values and help determine what is the "normal" value. This was done by recording doll dealers' selling prices, checking with collectors who have purchased the dolls shown to see what they paid for their items, interviewing both collectors and dealers to question them about values of these items, as well as checking online auction ending prices. If you ask 12 different collectors or dealers what an item is worth, you would probably receive 12 different answers. That happened to me on many occasions while trying to compile values for this book. I had a collector tell me she paid $150.00 for a doll, while a dealer told me that same doll was difficult to move and she couldn't get anyone to purchase it for more than $50.00. Other times, I had dealers tell me an item was worth two or three times more than what a collector would tell me they paid for the same item at a doll show. My job was to take those 12 different answers I received about the value of a doll and determine what was the norm. Since there really is no one set value for any collectible doll, I have provided a range of values. While this may confuse some people who want to know exactly how much their doll is worth, it is more realistic to have value listed this way. If a doll has flaws, it will be valued on the lower end or possibly even well below the listed value. If a doll is perfect, it would be valued on the higher end of the listed value. As confusing as it seems to some people, even mint-in-box values can vary depending on the condition of the box or original packaging. A doll can still be considered mint-in-box (MIB), even if the box is squashed with the cellophane coming off as long as the doll is undamaged or unflawed. If this were the case, the doll would be valued lower then the MIB value but higher than the mint and loose value.

In your collecting travels you may note people selling dolls for higher or lower than the values listed in this book. That will always be the case. I must stress there is really no one set value for a doll because at different times and through different sources different people will pay different amounts for the same item.

Unless otherwise specified, the values listed in this book are for dolls without their original boxes wearing their original clothing and in very good to excellent condition. If a doll is in played-with condition (i.e., messed up or thinning hair, dirty, makeup paint rubbed off, scratches in plastic or vinyl) or the doll is not dressed in his or her original clothing, value would be less than that listed. If a doll's hair has been cut, the value diminishes quite a bit and the doll could be worth less than half of the listed value. If the original box or packaging is included with the doll, value would be higher than the listed value and can be even higher if the box or packaging is unflawed in any way. All values listed in this book are based on the United States doll market and would vary for other countries based on supply and demand of each particular doll in that country.

Tippee Toes, see page 141 for more details.

Vermont Maid Doll: Premium doll offered in 1963 for $2.50 plus a bottle liner from the top of Vermont Maid Syrup. For $4.25 you could purchase the doll and three extra outfits, or the outfits could be purchased alone for $2.00. The Vermont Maid doll is 15" tall, marked "U/39," and believed to have been made by Uneeda. She is wearing her original dress, blouse, and shoes, but is missing her original hair ribbons. **$15.00 – 20.00.** *Courtesy Ann Wagner.*

Campbell's Bicentennial Kids: 10½" all vinyl dolls dressed in colonial outfits. The dolls were produced for Campbell's Soup in 1976 for America's bicentennial. Both the dolls and the clothing are unmarked. **$45.00 – 75.00 pair.** *Courtesy Ann Wagner.*

Alexander Doll Co.

Madame Alexander Dolls: Sears 1962 Christmas catalog shows some of the Madame Alexander dolls available at the time including Marybel, Kitten, Smarty, Bunny, and the Little Women set.

Marybel the get-well doll wants you for a little nurse

$11⁹⁸

15-inch doll has a cast to heal make-believe broken arms or legs; crutches just her size; dark glasses to wear when she's dotted with red measles; yellow spots for chicken pox. Band-aids and bandages for minor scratches. When little nurse removes her make-believe diseases and bandages, Marybel gets well right away.

She's exquisitely fashioned with rigid plastic body and is realistically tinted. Has jointed arms, legs. Turning waist and vinyl head. Her long-lashed eyes go to sleep and her lovely rooted Saran hair is distinctively styled. Rayon satin lace trimmed shortie pajamas, removable cotton fleecy slippers. Marybel has the fine workmanship like all Madame Alexander dolls. Packed complete in Fiberboard case.
49 N 3670—Shpg. wt. 3 lbs. 4 oz. ..$11.98

Cuddly "Kitten" now cries $8⁹⁸ .. poses naturally

19-inch do[l]

Who wouldn't be smitten with "Kitten"—this a[rm]ful of huggable softness. Her dimpled face with th[e] lashed, closing eyes will steal any little girl's he[art] Rooted plastic hair is done in wispy baby style. [Hold] her . . she'll cry softly.

Exquisitely made like all Madame Alexander d[olls] Kitten's pretty baby face, soft arms and legs [are] vinyl. Lightweight body is Kapok-filled cotton. [So] limp she flops into many poses . . you can put [a] finger into her mouth. "Kitten" comes wearing a [cot]ton shirt, plus diaper and a soft, nylon-tricot kim[ono]
49 N 3260—19-inch doll. Wt. 2 lbs. 12 oz. ...... $[
49 N 3247—14-inch doll. Wt. 1 lb. 12 oz. ....

Exquisite Dolls on this page made by *Madame Alexander*

$9⁴⁴ each

Famous Little Women

Louisa May Alcott's storybook heroines come to life. 12-inch plastic bodies have jointed arms and legs. Saran hair wigs are styled of that period. Turning heads have lashed, go-to-sleep eyes. All wear cotton pantalettes, crinolines, socks and shoes.

[1] **Meg.** Lacy cotton pinafore over colored cotton dress.
49 N 3653—Shipping weight each 1 pound......$9.44
[2] **Amy.** Cotton dress with frilly ruffled pinafore.
49 N 3649—Shipping weight each 1 pound...... 9.44
[3] **Jo.** Sedate Pin-dot cotton dress, cotton pinafore.
49 N 3658—Shipping weight each 1 pound...... 9.44
Beth (not shown). Polished cotton dress, contrasting trim.
49 N 3651—Shipping weight each 1 pound..........$9.44

Lovable 18-inch "Bunny" holds her hands out to mommy

$9⁵⁹

Looks as though she's ready to speak. A darling with great animation in her lovely smile and the way she holds her hands. Big, expressive moving eyes with lashes. Shining plastic hair is rooted and has pert rayon bow. Body, legs are jointed, lightweight, but durable plastic. Soft vinyl head, arms also move. "Bunny" wears a dotted Swiss cotton dress trimmed with organdy. Party slippers, socks.
49 N 3370—Shipping weight 2 lbs. 4 oz....... $9.59

$5⁸⁵   **$5⁸⁵**

12-inch Smarty is Queen of the May

These small Baby Dolls are so pop[ular] with little girls . . and big ones too!

[4] So saucy and sassy . . . fully jo[inted] doll just waiting to perk up your y[oung] lady. She's ready for a party dressed [in] flowered nylon dress. Wears party slip[pers] and socks. Lashed, moving eyes; [head] and arms of soft plastic, legs and bo[dy of] sturdy plastic. Rooted plastic hair.
49 N 3326—Shipping wt. 1 lb........

12-inch Smarty in Artist's Smock

[5] And what else would a young a[rtist] carry in her pocket but her p[aint] brush and crayon. She wears matc[hing] bloomers, slippers and socks. Sturdy [plas]tic body and jointed legs. Rooted plas[tic] hair in pixie style. Vinyl plastic [head] and arms move. Lashed, go-to-sleep [eyes]
49 N 3329—Shipping weight 1 lb.....

Quintuplets: These quintuplet dolls have been dubbed The Fischer Quints by collectors, although the name Fischer was not actually used by the Alexander Doll Company for the dolls. These dolls came out in 1964, the year following the birth of the Fischer babies, the first set of surviving quintuplets born in the U.S. The 7" dolls were made with the Little Genius face mold. MIB: **$175.00 – 245.00.** *Courtesy Hillary and Cliff James, Toy With Me.*

Hungarian: 7½" bent knee Hungarian from the International series. The Hungarian doll was available for many years but this particular doll was purchased in the early 1970s. She is marked "ALEX" on her back. Her vest is tagged "Hungarian/by MADAME ALEXANDER®/NEW YORK, U.S.A." Played with condition, no box: **$20.00 – 35.00.**

Betsy McCall: 8" Betsy McCall wearing her B-129 Sugar and Spice outfit. Doll and outfit: **$175.00 – 225.00.** *Courtesy Karen Hickey.*

Betsy McCall: Several different companies made Betsy McCall dolls in various sizes. Shown here is an 8" Betsy McCall by American Character wearing B-59 Holiday dress (missing hat, tights, shoes). Doll wearing Betsy McCall dress: **$175.00 – 225.00.**

Betsy McCall: 8" Betsy McCall wearing outfit #9203 Birthday Party. The case she is carrying is a miniature reproduction of a Betsy McCall pretty pac. Doll and outfit: **$175.00 – 225.00.** *Courtesy Karen Hickey.*

Betsy McCall: Sears 1963 Christmas Catalog shows only a few of the many outfits that were available for the 8" Betsy McCall doll.

Betsy McCall: A 14" Betsy McCall shown with an 8" Betsy, both wearing Town and Country. The 14" doll on the left is wearing 14E (missing beret) and the 8" doll on the right is wearing B-42. 14" doll: **$175.00 – 275.00.** 8" doll: **$175.00 – 225.00.** *Courtesy Karen Hickey.*

Betsy McCall: Two 14" Betsy McCall dolls. The 14" size Betsy was produced in 1958 and 1959. The dolls are marked "McCall/ 19©58/Corp." The doll on the left is wearing 14E Town and Country (missing beret) and the doll on the right is wearing 14F Formal (minus the nylon tricot stole). Doll in Town and Country: **$175.00 – 275.00.** Doll in Formal: **$175.00 – 275.00.** *Courtesy Karen Hickey.*

Betsy McCall: This 22" Betsy McCall doll from 1962 came dressed in several different outfits including the one shown here. The doll is jointed at the neck, shoulders, wrists, waist, hips, thighs, and ankles. MIB: **$250.00 – 300.00.** *Courtesy Kathleen Tornikoski, Romancing the Doll.*

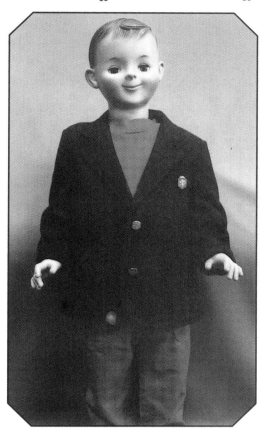

Sandy McCall: A 36" Betsy McCall doll was issued by American Character during the time when Ideal's Patti Playpal and other child-sized dolls were popular. Sandy McCall was Betsy McCall's cousin and he was issued in a 38" Playpal-sized doll. He was advertised as being life sized and could wear real little boy's clothing. Sandy is marked "McCall Corp./1959" on his head. The doll in the photo has been re-dressed. Re-dressed doll: **$200.00 – 250.00.**

Whimsies: First appearing in 1961, the Whimsies had molded heads and bodies that were one-piece stuffed vinyl. Their 19" to 21" size makes collecting the whole set difficult for those with limited space. Whimsie dolls include the following: Annie the Astronaut, Betty the Beauty (wears banner reading "Miss Take"), Bessie the Bashful Bride, Dixie the Pixie, Fanny the Flapper, Fanny the Fallen Angel, Lena the Cleaner, Hedda Get Bedda (three-faced doll with knob on top of head), Hilda the Hillbilly (called Raggie in a 1961 American Character brochure), Monk or Friar (name unknown), Polly the Lolly, Simon the Degree (graduate), Samson the Strongman, Suzie the Snoozie, Trixie the Pixie (dressed like devil), Tillie the Talker, Wheeler the Dealer, Zack the Sack, and Zero the Hero (football player). Whimsies' marks vary slightly, but some dolls are marked "Whimsies/19©60/AMER.DOLL.& TOY (all in circle)" on their heads and "AMER DOLL & TOY CORP./19©60" on their backs. The photos show Lena the Cleaner in her original box. MIB: **$175.00 – 250.00.** *Courtesy Sharon Wendrow, Memory Lane.*

Tressy: 11½" Tressy with her "magic" growing hair strand was a novelty in the teenage fashion doll world. When the button on her stomach is pushed and her growing hair strand is pulled, Tressy's hair grows. When a "T" shaped key is inserted in a slot in her back her hair goes short again. Although Tressy was only available in the U.S. from 1963 through 1967, she was very popular in other countries throughout the 1970s and 1980s. She was manufactured by Bella under license from American Character Toy Company in France, Palitoy in England, and Regal Toy Ltd. in Canada. In Germany Tressy was called Kessy. Although companies other than American Character produced Tressy for other countries, the foreign Tressy dolls are included under this section to keep them together. Values for Tressy can vary from one example to the next. Collectors will pay higher for a prettier or more unusual example of a doll than they will for one that is fairly common in appearance.

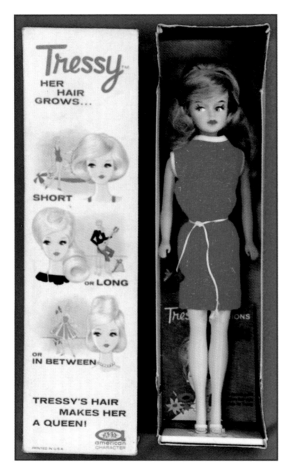

Tressy: 11½" straight leg Tressy in her original box. The doll is marked "AMERICAN DOLL & TOY CORP./19©63" in a circle on her head. Sometimes markings are hidden underneath her hairline. MIB: **$75.00 – 100.00.**

Tressy: Tressy wearing her #15902 Sophisticated Lady dress (also came in maroon). She is marked "AMERICAN DOLL & TOY CORP./19©63" in a circle on her head. With dress: **$30.00 – 40.00.**

Tressy: A bright blond Tressy with unusually long hair. She has the same markings as the doll above. She is wearing an unknown vintage dress but the hat she is wearing is from a pink version of her #20905 Evening Jewel outfit (also came in yellow). Loose Tressy dolls wearing generic outfits often range about $15.00 – 35.00, but exceptionally pretty examples such as this one would run higher: **$30.00 – 50.00.**

Posing Tressy: This Tressy gift set included a blond Posing Tressy doll with her extra #25900 Hootenanny outfit inside a cardboard Tressy carrying case. The doll in the gift set was found wearing Ideal Tammy's original jumpsuit, but she was probably re-dressed by someone somewhere along the way as other examples of similar gift sets have Tressy dressed in one of her own dresses. The posing doll has wires inside her legs, allowing them to bend and pose. Gift set complete with NRFC outfit: **$125.00 – 200.00.** *Courtesy Janet Lawrence and Mike Lawrence.*

Tressy: A rare black version of Tressy was also produced by American Character. She came with either straight or posing legs. Shown in the photo is a straight leg black Tressy wearing her terrycloth cover-up from #30902 In the Swim. **$275.00 – 350.00.**

Tressy: Another straight leg black Tressy wearing a red and white version of her #15903 Neat Knit dress (missing belt). The Neat Knit dress also came in a black and red version. **$275.00 – 350.00.** *Courtesy Dal Lowenbein.*

Tressy: This French Tressy was made by Bella in the 1970s, possibly into the 1980s. She has a plastic torso with a "grow hair" button in the middle, a vinyl head and vinyl limbs. She is slightly taller than the American Tressy measuring 12" and her head is larger than the U.S. dolls. Her plastic stand has a slot where her hair key is kept. She is marked "BELLA/31·14" on her head. MIB: **$55.00 – 75.00.**

Tressy: 12" Bella Tressy wearing an outfit sold separately for her. **$35.00 – 45.00.**

Tressy: Back of Bella Tressy's box showing some of the outfits available for her as well as her sister Cathie.

Tressy: 12" Bella Tressy in her original box. MIB: **$55.00 – 75.00.** *Courtesy Janet and Mike Lawrence.*

Tressy: Four different Bella Tressy dolls wearing Tressy outfits sold separately for her. **$35.00 – 45.00 each.** *Courtesy Janet and Mike Lawrence.*

Tressy: This Palitoy Tressy was made for the British market and is believed to be from the late 1970s, possibly into the 1980s. The 11" Palitoy Tressy has jointed wrists, hands that can grip objects, and bendable elbows and knees. Her hair grows with a button on her torso, but her back has a knob that winds to shorten her hair once again instead of using a key as many Tressy dolls need. She is marked "35/PALITOY/12" on her head and ALL COPYRIGHT RESERVED/C.P.G. PRODUCTS CORP./TRESSY®/ MADE IN HONG KONG" on her back. She is wearing the U.S. version #20902 Summer Holiday outfit. Doll with outfit: **$35.00 – 50.00.**

Bellita, Miss Bella, or Tressy: This doll was sold in France around 1965 under the name Bellita or Miss Bella. She has straight legs and is 11½" tall. She has the same face as Snouky, the French version of Cricket who was also made in 1965. In researching this doll, the author found conflicting information about her. Some believe Bellita or Miss Bella dolls were not made with growing hair, but others say they were also available in a growing hair version. One source indicated that some of these dolls have been found in boxes calling her Tressy, Miss Bella. None of these statements could be proven true or false at the time of publication. The doll here is shown wearing Tressy's Majorette outfit from 1966 which was made for the European market. Doll only: **$50.00 – 65.00.** Outfit only: **$55.00 – 75.00.**

Tressy's fashions were sold either in boxed sets called, High Fashions or on hanging cards called Budget Fashions. The boxed sets were better quality clothing and in addition to the outfit itself often contained several small accessories. Often times one article of clothing in the set was tagged with a woven Tressy T.M." label. Tressy's Budget Fashions were inferior in quality to the High Fashion outfits. Sometimes pieces from the Budget Fashions have a paper tag that reads Made in Hong Kong." However not all the pieces to the outfit have the tag and often the paper tag falls off so when loose these Budget Fashion pieces are hard to identify as Tressy's for those not familiar with them. The Budget Fashions seemed to have been made with whatever material happened to be available at the time, because many of them have been spotted in different colors or made with different fabrics.

Tressy Fashion: The outfit in the photo is Budget Fashion #10900 Summer Time. This dress has been found in a blue flower print as well. NRFP: **$35.00 – 45.00.**

Tressy Fashion: Budget Fashion #10903 Good News. NRFP: **$40.00 – 55.00.**

Tressy Fashion: Budget Fashion #10901 Bewitching shown in black and blue. NRFP: **$45.00 – 55.00.**

Tressy Fashion: Another Budget Fashion #10911 Date Mates. This outfit has been found in several different colors. NRFP: **$35.00 – 45.00.**

Cricket: Tressy's 9" little sister in the U.S was called Cricket. Cricket started life as Tressy's little cousin but later was changed to Tressy's little sister. The earliest Cricket dolls are the ones with waist-long straight hair with bangs. These dolls came with either blue or brown eyes. Like Tressy, Cricket enjoyed a long life in Europe. In France Tressy's little sister was called Snouky and in England she was called Toots. The photo shows a blue-eyed Cricket wearing #14101, Ship Ahoy and a brown-eyed Cricket wearing #14201 Bowling Beauty, two outfits sold separately for her. The dolls are marked "AMER. CHAR. INC/19©64" on the back of their heads. **$25.00 – 45.00 each.** *Courtesy Rebecca Wingler.*

Cricket: This Cricket doll has the growing hair feature like her sister Tressy. The doll in the photo is wearing her #14104 Party Pretty dress. She is marked "AMER. CHAR. INC/19©64" on the back of her head. **$20.00 – 35.00.**

Cricket Fashion: Like her sister Tressy, Cricket fashions were sold either in boxed sets or on hanging cards. Shown in the photo is her #14100 Fun and Fancy outfit. NRFP: **$25.00 – 45.00.**

Cricket Fashion: #14101 Ship-Ahoy. NRFP: **$25.00 – 45.00.**

Cricket Fashion: #14102 Windy Weather. NRFP: **$25.00 – 45.00.**

Cricket Fashion: #14103 Sweet Treat. NRFP: **$25.00 – 45.00.**

Cricket Fashion: #14104 Party Pretty. The flower on the dress came in varying shades of pink or lavender. NRFP: **$25.00 – 45.00.**

Cricket Fashion: #14105 Just Pals. NRFP: **$25.00 – 45.00.**

Cricket Fashion: #14106 Happy Hobby. NRFP: **$25.00 – 45.00.**

Cricket Fashion: #14107 Mad Music. NRFP: **$25.00 – 45.00.**

Cricket Fashion: #14108 Shutter-Bug. NRFP: **$25.00 – 45.00.**

Cathie: Bella was the company who issued Tressy in France and possibly other parts of Europe. In addition to Tressy, Bella produced a big sister for her named Cathie, whose size was a bit out of proportion with the 12" Tressy doll. Beginning in 1967 Cathie dolls were about 17½" then after 1980 she was a little over 19" tall. The grow-hair version of Cathie had long rooted hair and a grow hair strand that worked by pressing a button on her belly to make it grow and a knob on her back to wind the hair short. Cathie's hair came in golden blond, ash blond, auburn, and brunette. Her hair came styled with a center or side part or with bangs. She had either hazel, blue, or green sleep eyes and rooted lashes. The photo shows two Cathie dolls wearing two of her fashions. **$45.00 – 65.00 each.** *Courtesy Janet and Mike Lawrence.*

Cathie: A brunette Bella Cathie doll. **$45.00 – 65.00.** *Courtesy Janet and Mike Lawrence.*

Cathie: Another brunette Bella Cathie doll. Note the "Bella" tag on the bottom of her dress. **$45.00 – 65.00.** *Courtesy Janet and Mike Lawrence.*

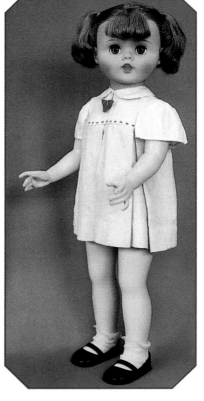

Little Miss Echo: With the help of a continuous magnetic tape inside her, Little Miss Echo repeats whatever is said to her when the knob on her chest is turned. She was issued in different sizes, with different hair colors and styles, and wearing different outfits. The 28½" Little Miss Echo in the photo is wearing her original dress. She is marked "PAT. PEND" on the battery compartment cover on her stomach. **$95.00 – 125.00.**

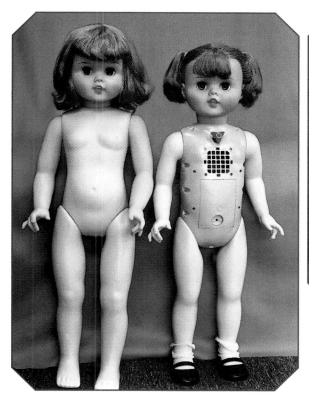

Little Miss Echo-type doll: The author has not been able to identify the doll on the left in this photo. She is basically the same doll as Little Miss Echo but she does not have the talking mechanism in her torso. She measures 30" while the Miss Echo in the photo measures 28½". The non-talking doll in the photo was purchased without clothing so it is unknown what her original outfit was. She is marked "26" on the back of her head and S" on her lower torso. The doll on the right has no markings on her. 30" doll: **$55.00 – 65.00.**

Tiny Tears: Tiny Tears doll was a popular seller throughout the 1950s and continued on in various versions through the 1960s into the 1970s. Over the years, the materials used on the dolls changed from a rubber body with a hard plastic head to a vinyl body with a hard plastic head and finally to an all vinyl doll. In the 1960s the famous Tiny Tears name was expanded to include Teeny Tiny Tears, Teeny Weenie Tiny Tears, Baby Tiny Tears, and Lifesize Tiny Tears. The photo shows a 16" all vinyl Tiny Tears circa 1964. The doll is marked "19©64/AMER.CHAR.DOLL." on head. The doll is not wearing her original outfit. In the background is a 1965 Tiny Tears record album by Majorette Records. Doll: **$25.00 – 35.00.** Album: **$10.00 – 15.00.**

Teeny Tiny Tears/Teenie Weenie Tiny Tears: Two 12" Teeny Tiny Tears and an 8½" Teenie Weenie Tiny Tears are shown with the same Tiny Tears record album shown with the 16" doll above. The 12" dolls are marked "AM. CHAR.©" on their heads and the 8½" doll is marked "19©64/AMER. CHAR. DOLL" on her head. **$15.00 – 30.00 each.**

Teeny Tiny Tears: Here is a rare black version of Teeny Tiny Tears, circa 1963. The 12" vinyl doll is marked "AM. CHAR.©" on her head. It is unknown for sure if the outfit she is wearing is a Teeny Tiny Tears outfit. **$45.00 – 60.00.** *Courtesy Robin Englehart, vintagelane.com, photo by Nancy Jean Mong.*

Teenie Weenie Tiny Tears: This 8½" version of Tiny Tears is shown with some of the clothing sold separately for her. The doll is marked "19©64/AMER.CHAR.DOLL" on her head. She is wearing her original outfit. Doll: **$15.00 – 25.00.** Loose outfits: **$3.00 – 10.00 each.**

Tiny Tears has rockabye eyes—rock her and watch her eyes, they slowly close as she goes to sleep!

[1] **TEENY TINY TEARS** is the cuddly, lifelike baby doll that cries real tears, wets her diaper, drinks from a bottle, sleeps—and even blows bubbles! Her petal-soft vinyl plastic skin loves a bath. Rooted, pixie-style saran hair is fun to shampoo. Pastel colored dress. 12 in. tall. Pacifier, bottle, bubble pipe are included.
X 921-7332 A—1 lb. 5 oz. **3.88**

[2] **TEENIE WEENIE TINY TEARS.** Rock-a-bye eyes. Cries real tears, drinks from a bottle, sleeps, wets just as her big sister, Teeny Tiny Tears, does. Vinyl plastic body and rooted saran hair. Give her a bath if you like—she's washable, too. Includes pacifier, bottle. 9 in. tall. Pastel colored romper outfit.
X 921-7340 A—Wt. 12 oz. **2.88**

[3] **TEENY TINY TEARS AND TRUNK.** She has her own special travel trunk. Includes "A"-line dress, panties, extra diaper, besides dressed doll, bottle, pacifier and bubble pipe.
X 921-7381 A—2½ lbs... **7.77**

[4] **BATH TIME.*** Polka-dot bathrobe and matching towel. Also a sponge and shampoo for Teeny. Bottle, pacifier, pipe not incl.
X 921-3489 A—Wt. 6 oz.. **2.37**
Same, but for Teenie Weenie [2].
X 921-3497 A—Wt. 4 oz.. **1.57**

[5] **TRAVEL TIME.*** Teeny keeps warm in her set of knitted sweater, leggings, and bonnet. With "magic" sponge and shampoo. Bottle, pacifier, pipe not included.
X 921-3463 A—Wt. 6 oz.. **2.37**
Same, but for Teenie Weenie [2].
X 921-3430 A—Wt. 4 oz.. **1.57**

[6] **SUNDAY BEST.*** Teeny loves to dress up in her cotton frock and bonnet, panties. "Magic" sponge and shampoo. Rattle, socks not included.
X 921-7357 A—Wt. 6 oz.. **2.77**
Same, but for Teenie Weenie [2].
X 921-7365 A—Wt. 5 oz.. **1.57**

*Dolls not included.
Costumes from Japan.

[2] **2⁸⁸**
[1] **3⁸⁸**

[4] **2.37** [5] **2.37** [6] **2.77**

[3] **7.77**

Rock ME

18″ cradle with 17″ doll
[7] **16.88**

Talking cradles include dolls!

13″ cradle with 12″ doll

TALK
[8] **14.88**

[7] **17-IN. TINY TEARS IN TALKING CRADLE.** Just slip in record—you'll hear nursery rhymes, prayers, lullabies. Includes doll in pajamas, bunting, mattress and cover, bottle, pacifier, bubble pipe, 6 records.
X 921-7399 A—5 lbs.... **16.88**
Same, but talking cradle, mattress, cover, and 6 records only (no doll).
X 921-7407 A—2½ lbs... **9.88**

[8] **12-IN. TEENY TINY TEARS IN TALKING CRADLE.** You'll listen to many lifelike phrases. Cradle has white mattress cover. Doll in pajama set and bunting. Includes 6 records, bottle, pacifier, bubble pipe. 2 lbs. 12 oz.
X 921-7415 A.......... **14.88**
12-in. Talking Cradle. As above, but without doll and bunting.
X 921-7423 A—2 lbs..... **8.88**

8.99
17″ doll and layette

Tiny Tears

"Which pretty outfit shall I wear today?"

TINY TEARS AND LAYETTE. 17-in. favorite with rockaby eyes. She cries real tears, drinks, wets, sleeps, and blows bubbles. Includes a pretty party dress, plus an adorable playsuit with a bow in the back, matching elasticized panties, socks, and bootees. Bottle, pacifier and bubble pipe, too. All for such a low price!
X 921-7373 A—Shpg. wt. 4 lbs.. **8.99**

SAVE THIS CATALOG—order toys till Sept. 20, 1966

PENNEY 237

Tiny Tears: This page from J.C. Penney 1965 Christmas catalog shows some of the different-sized Tiny Tears dolls including Teeny Tiny Tears and Teenie Weenie Tiny Tears.

"Let's whisper
Pst, Pst, Pst."

"Let's play
school."

DOLLS that TALK

Push a button and
"Terri Talks"
she walks with you when you
guide her
$10⁰⁰

6

Baby Secret
Whispers to you . . .
her lips move, too
SEEN ON
TV $8⁸⁸

[5] "LET ME WHISPER IN YOUR EAR"—Baby
Secret wants to share her secrets with you
—pull the "Magic Ring" and she whispers
in her ever-so-wee baby voice and her lips
move realistically. Soft, bendable foam body,
wears flannel pj's. About 18 in. tall.
48 HT 10001—Ship. wt. 2 lbs. 12 oz..... $8.88

[6] TERRI AND HER MOMMY CAN HAVE A LIVELY CON-
VERSATION as they walk along together. Simply
push a button and Terri repeats 9 sentences. 18-in.
toddler with chubby cheeks, soft rooted hair, moving eyes, fully jointed vinyl. Wears A-line dress,
panties, shoes. Uses 1 "D" cell, sold on Pg. 370.
48 HT 10028—Ship. wt. 2 lbs. 8 oz........... $10.00

Baby Cheryl recites her
favorite nursery rhymes
$7⁶⁷

[7] CUDDLESOME BABY CHERYL likes to show off for
everyone—just pull the "Magic Ring," she
says "Jack and Jill"... other lines at random in
baby talk. Wears dress, panties, booties. Stuffed
body, rooted hair, moving eyes. Abt. 16 in.
48 HT 10029—Ship. wt. 1 lb. 8 oz.......... $7.67

Baby Colleen . . .
So Soft . . . Endearing
$6⁹⁵

[8] SURE 'N SHE'S SUCH A GOOD GIRL even with
her mischievous look—pull her "Magic
Ring": she says 11 different bedtime sentences.
Soft body, vinyl arms, head, saucy rooted red
hair. Wears nightie, she can be dressed.
48 HT 10040—Abt. 15 in. Ship. wt. 2 lbs..... $6.95

"Can you move
your lips?"

"Jack and
Jill went up
the hill . . ."

7

8

"Tell me a
long, long
story."

9

Baby Teenietalk
her lips move as she talks
$8⁸⁸

[9] NEW BABY TEENIETALK sounds just like a baby learn-
ing to talk—you've seen her on TV. Her lips move
as she says 11 sentences. Cuddly, lovable, has rooted
hair, vinyl arms, head. Wears dress, slip, panties, booties.
48 HT 10002—About 17 in. tall.
Ship. wt. 3 lbs. 3 oz..... $8.88   ACFKD WARDS 231

Terri Talks: Montgomery Wards 1966 Christmas catalog showing Terri Talks. Note the resemblance of her original dress to the Teeny Tiny Tears dress shown inside the carrying case in the J.C. Penney 1965 catalog pictured on the previous page. Sears 1966 Christmas catalog pictured a Terri Talks doll wearing a different dress.

Terri Talks: This battery-operated 18" doll has a vinyl head with blue sleep eyes and a hard plastic body. She is marked "Amer. Char. Doll/19©63." The proper spelling of this doll's name is unknown. Montgomery Wards 1966 Christmas catalog spelled Terri with an i" while the 1966 Sears Christmas catalog spelled Terry with a y." **$55.00 – 65.00.** *Courtesy Ann Wagner.*

Pouting Penny: 12" doll that frowns when her arm is lowered. She has brown painted eyes and freckles. Penny is marked "AMER.CHAR.INC. /19©66" on her neck. The doll in the photo is not wearing her original outfit. Re-dressed doll: **$15.00 – 20.00.**

Arrow Rubber & Plastic Corporation

aka Arrow Industries Inc.

Arrow Rubber & Plastics Corporation, also doing business as Arrow Industries, Inc., manufactured a large number of rubber squeak toys, including dolls, animals, and character figures designed by The Edward Mobley Company. Some of the animals Arrow made came with open and shut doll eyes, while others had painted eyes. Often the neck of the animal was jointed allowing the head to turn.

Rags: This 9½" tall and 7" long squeaker dog was advertised under the name Rags. He has open and shut eyes and a jointed neck. He is marked "©THE EDWARD MOBLEY CO. 1964/MFG. BY 2 1964/ ©ARROW INDUSTRIES INC." on his head and "©THE EDWARD MOBLEY CO. 1964/8/MFG BY / ©ARROW INDUSTRIES INC." on the bottom. **$15.00 – 20.00.**

Bowser Wowser: 10½" tall and 10" long vinyl squeaker dog with cloth ears. His red collar has a yellow dog tag with his name carved intaglio on it, "BOWSER WOWSER." He has open and shut eyes and a jointed neck. Bowser Wowser is marked "PATENT PENDING/©THE EDWARD MOBLEY CO. 1969/MFG BY THE ARROW RUBBER & PLASTIC CORP." on his head and "©THE EDWARD MOBLEY CO. 1969/MFG BY/THE ARROW RUBBER & PLASTIC CORP." on the bottom. **$20.00 – 25.00.**

Cat: 9" tall and 8½" long, this squeaker cat has open and shut eyes and a jointed neck. He is marked "©THE EDWARD MOBLEY CO. 1960/MFG. BY ARROW RUBBER & PLASTICS CORP." on the bottom. **$15.00 – 20.00.**

Cat: Same cat as on page 28, except tinted blue. This cat is also 9" tall and 8½" long and has the same markings. **$15.00 – 20.00.** *Courtesy Ann Wagner.*

Rabbit: 11" tall and 9½" long vinyl squeaker rabbit. He has open and shut eyes and a jointed neck. He is marked "©THE EDWARD MOBLEY CO. 1961/MFG. BY THE ARROW RUBBER & PLASTIC CORP." on his head and "©THE EDWARD MOBLEY CO. 1961/MFG. BY/THE ARROW RUBBER & PLASTIC CORP." on the bottom. **$15.00 – 20.00.**

Brooks-Melrose

Raggie Maggie: This 14" country girl rag doll has no date on the doll or box, but most likely came out during the mid-1970s when American Greeting Company's Holly Hobbie was at the height of popularity. Mint with box: **$20.00 – 25.00.** *Courtesy Robin Englehart, vintagelane.com, photo by Nancy Jean Mong.*

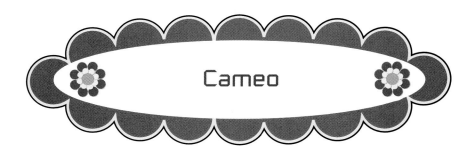
Joseph L. Kallus was founder and owner of Cameo Doll Products Company. He sculpted many of the dolls that came from his company including Rose O'Neill's Kewpie dolls. Joseph Kallus began assisting Rose O'Neill in the development of Kewpie dolls sometime around 1916 and his company continued producing the dolls through the 1960s. Over the years Kewpie dolls were made of bisque, composition, celluloid, and other materials but by the 1960s many of the Kewpie dolls being made or licensed by Cameo were vinyl. Remco, Jesco, and Amsco (a division of Milton Bradley) were just some of the companies that sold vinyl Kewpie dolls under license by Cameo. When not in their original boxes it's hard to determine which company put out which dolls as most of the dolls were only marked "Cameo" and did not have markings of the doll company that sold them.

Kewpie Girl: A girl with unusual long molded hair. She is 13½" and all vinyl. The doll is marked "on the back of her head "JLK" off to the left side, "©CAMEO" in the center, and "2/4" off to the right side of that. On her back she is marked "©CAMEO." The doll has a squeaker in her stomach. Her clothing is all original. **$65.00 – 95.00.**

Kewpie: 13" vinyl doll with pink dress and flowered apron. She is marked "S4-/14" on the left side of the back of her head, "1965" in the center, and off to the right side of that "JLK." Under those markings on her neck is "©CAMEO." On her back she is also marked "©CAMEO." Her head and body both squeak when squeezed. Although she is marked "1965," this doll was shown in the Montgomery Wards 1968 Christmas catalog. Her clothing is all original. **$25.00 – 40.00.**

Kewpie: 8" vinyl girl with a squeaker in her stomach. She is marked "6⅛" behind her right ear, "JLK" off to the left side of her head, and "©CAMEO" under her molded hairline. On her back she is marked "©CAMEO." It is believed she was manufactured by Remco Industries. The doll in the photo is all original except missing her shoes. Loose doll: **$15.00 – 25.00.**

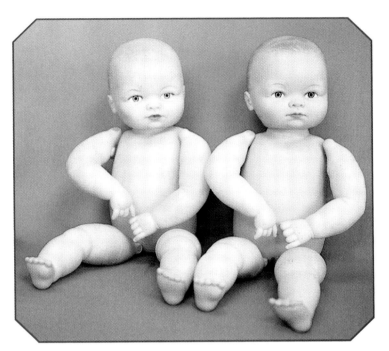

Kewpie: 7" all vinyl doll that squeaks when squeezed. The Kewpie is marked "52" above his molded hair line in the back of his head, "JLK" off to the side of his head, and "©CAMEO" under his molded hairline. The doll's original clothing included a blue blouse and polka dot pants. Although licensed by Cameo Doll Products, the doll was put out by Remco Industries in 1968. Loose/no box: **$10.00 – 15.00.**

Miss Peep/Baby Wendy: Sculpted by Joseph L. Kallus, Miss Peep is vinyl with molded hair and beautiful inset eyes. Her unique shoulder pin-joints allow her arms to rotate completely around as well as move back and forth. Her leg joints allow a back-and-forth movement. In 1973 Montgomery Wards sold a Miss Peep doll under the name Baby Wendy. Baby Wendy has an open mouth with a nursing hole in the center, unlike Miss Peep who has a closed mouth. Both dolls are marked "S.I.GIC263" on the under portion of the torso. In addition, Miss Peep on the right is marked "CAMEO©" on her head and back while Baby Wendy on the left does not have the CAMEO markings. Miss Peep is 18" and Baby Wendy is 16½". Nude: **$50.00 – 75.00.**

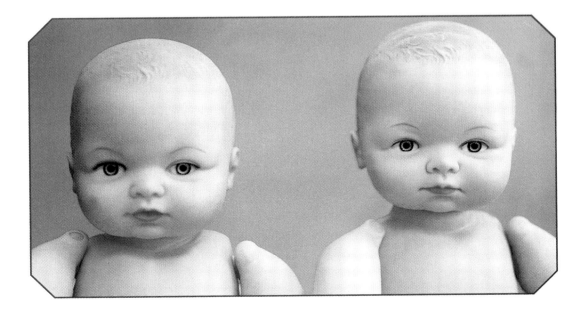

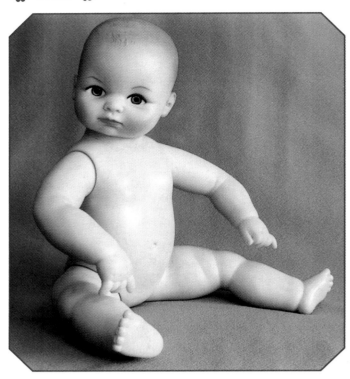

Miss Peep: Here is a 14" doll with jointed arms and legs rather than the hinged limbs like the previous dolls. Her legs, arms, and head are made of a hard vinyl while her torso is a softer vinyl. She is marked "©CAMEO" on her head and "16" on her back. Under her right arm there is the number "22" and under her left arm is "7." Circa 1976. Nude: **$20.00 – 30.00.**

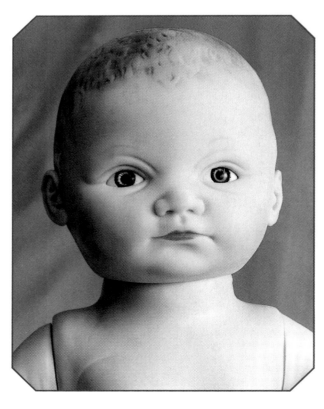

Unknown Cameo Doll: This doll has been called Newborn Peep in some reference books, but the author couldn't find any company reference to verify that name for sure. The 17½" doll has inset glass eyes similar to Miss Peep with jointed arms and a one-piece vinyl torso with stuffed vinyl legs. The doll has a squeaker inside her torso so when the doll is squeezed she cries or squeaks. The doll is marked "©/CAMEO" on the head and "10" on the back. **$25.00 – 35.00.**

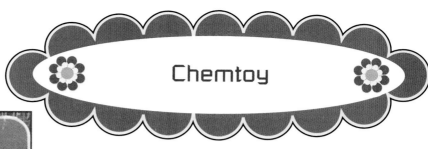

John Travolta: 12" doll from 1977 made in the image of actor John Travolta. MIB: **$45.00 – 75.00.** *Courtesy Sharon Criscione.*

Miss Cindy: Back of Cragstan's Miss Cindy box.

Miss Cindy: Fans of Deluxe Reading's Penny Brite doll will recognize the similarities between Cragstan's Miss Cindy doll and Penny Brite. The 8" Miss Cindy is marked "HONG KONG" on her head and back. She has a soft vinyl head and soft plastic torso and limbs. Doll with box: **$20.00 – 25.00.** Doll only: **$5.00 – 10.00.**

Miss Cindy/Penny Brite: Miss Cindy on the left is shown next to Deluxe Reading's Penny Brite. Like so many other dolls made in Hong Kong. Miss Cindy is of inferior quality to Penny Brite, but she makes a nice addition to any Penny Brite fan's collection.

Little Miss Mod Fun Fashion Jewelry: This jewelry set put out by Cragstan was most likely available from the mid to late 1960s. The package states "Made in The British Crown Colony of Hong Kong." The set includes a watch, a charm bracelet, and two earrings. Doll in the bracelet measures approximately 2¾" while the other three dolls measure approximately 2½". MIP: **$25.00 – 35.00.**

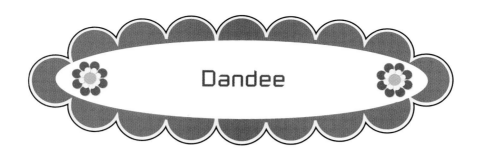
Fashion World Doll: Collectors of Topper's Dawn doll will notice the strong resemblance of this doll to Dawn. Like Dawn, the Fashion World doll is 6½" and has rooted eyelashes. There is no specific doll name on the box, only an item number, 1257. MIB: **$25.00 – 30.00.** *Courtesy Robin Englehart, vintagelane.com, photo by Nancy Jean Mong.*

Fashion World Clothes: This outfit looks quite similar to Dawn's Groovy Baby Groovy outfit. All the Fashion World outfits had item numbers but no names. Sometimes two or three different outfits shared the same item number. The outfits were made in British Hong Kong. Item number of this outfit is unknown. NRFP: **$10.00 – 15.00.** *Courtesy Robin Englehart, vintagelane.com, photo by Nancy Jean Mong.*

Fashion World Clothes: Item number 1205, red and silver dress. NRFP: **$10.00 – 15.00.** *Courtesy Robin Englehart, vintagelane.com, photo by Nancy Jean Mong.*

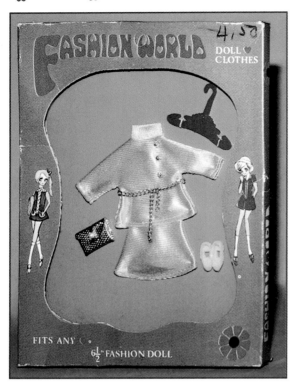

Fashion World Clothes: Item number unknown, yellow belted top and skirt. NRFP: **$10.00 – 15.00.**
Courtesy Robin Englehart, vintagelane.com, photo by Nancy Jean Mong.

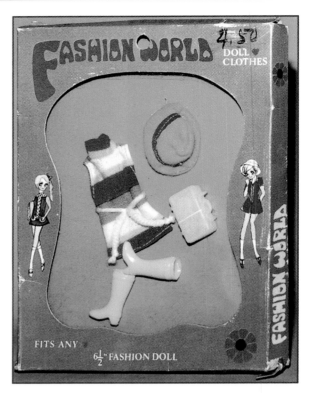

Fashion World Clothes: Item number 1625, multi-colored mini dress with hat. NRFP: **$10.00 – 15.00.**
Courtesy Robin Englehart, vintagelane.com, photo by Nancy Jean Mong.

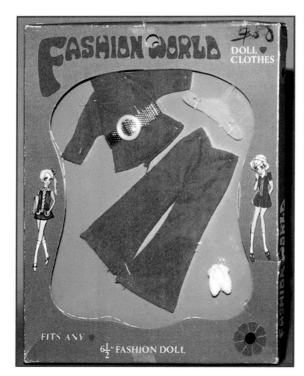

Fashion World Clothes: Item number 1207, orange top and slacks. NRFP: **$10.00 – 15.00.** *Courtesy Robin Englehart, vintagelane.com, photo by Nancy Jean Mong.*

Little Miss Fashion Doll: The date this doll was available is unknown. It's possible she was sold in the late 1950s or into the early 1960s. It is believed she was sold only in supermarkets. Even though she might be considered a 1950s doll, she is included here so that those 1960s children who played with her or those collectors who come across her in their travels will know who she is. Little Miss Fashion Doll came with four complete outfits, a party outfit, a cowgirl ensemble, a pajama set, and a snow suit. MIB with all clothing: **$100.00 – 150.00.** *Courtesy Robin Englehart, vintagelane.com, photos by Nancy Jean Mong.*

Suzy Smart: School girl Suzy Smart is 24" with jointed knees and a talking mechanism in her torso. She has bright blond hair and originally was dressed in a red, green, and black plaid skirt with straps and attached slip, a white blouse, and a beret on her head. She came with a school desk and a blackboard on an easel. The doll in the photo is marked "319" on the back of her head, while another example of Suzy Smart was marked "490." Suzy's only other markings are on the battery compartment on her back that says "REMOVE TO REPLACE 'D' SIZE BATTERY" and "ON/OFF" next to her power button. No company name is on the doll. Many people have seen this doll, but do not know who she is. For this reason, she has been difficult for collectors to locate and so selling prices for her have been high. As more people learn who she is and more examples of Suzy Smart turn up on the collectors market, her value may go down some, but at the time of publication this doll's sale price is running high. Like many Deluxe Reading dolls, it is believed Suzy Smart was sold only in supermarkets, not in department stores or through catalogs. The Suzy Smart in the photo is wearing her original outfit, but is missing her beret. Doll without desk: **$65.00 – 95.00.**

Deluxe Beauty Parlor Doll: Deluxe Reading used the Suzy Smart face on this 24" doll which was sold in a set called Deluxe Beauty Parlor. The unnamed doll is basically the same doll as Suzy Smart but has dirty blond hair instead of bright blond and she does not have the talking mechanism in her torso. Like Suzy she has jointed knees. The doll was originally sold with a swivel beauty parlor chair, a hair dryer, and hair and manicure accessories. The doll in the photo is wearing her original dress, but it is unknown if her socks and shoes are original. Loose examples of this doll have been found wearing black shoes, as well as white. The doll's hair ribbon is not original. **$45.00 – 65.00.**

Deluxe Beauty Parlor Doll: Two different Deluxe Beauty Parlor dolls. The doll on the left has a smaller head then the doll on the right. The doll on the left is marked "D3/234" on her neck. The marks on the doll on the right are located much higher on the neck inside the hair and are illegible but are definitely different then the markings on the other doll. **$45.00 – 65.00 each.**

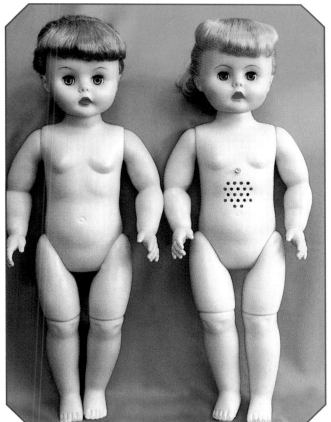

Suzy Smart and Deluxe Beauty Parlor Doll: Suzy Smart on the right is shown next to the Deluxe Beauty Parlor doll on the left. Other than their hair coloring and the talking mechanism in Suzy's torso, the two dolls are the same.

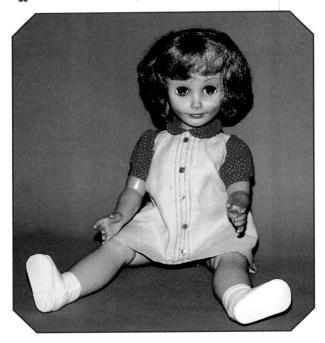

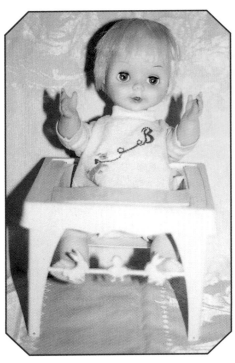

Baby Brite: 13½" doll whose head turns or arms rise when the button on her stomach is pressed. Baby Brite is marked "36/ Deluxe Reading/ ©1963/15.ME#H." Her nursery included a baby tender, crib, and bathinette. Her baby tender shown in the photo is marked "Cat. No./ Made by Deluxe Reading Corpora-tion/Elizabethport, New Jersey/U. S. of America." Doll with tender: **$25.00 – 35.00.** *Courtesy Ann Wagner.*

Suzy Homemaker: 22" with blue sleep eyes and joint-ed knees. She is marked "Deluxe Reading Corp./19©64/64." **$20.00 – 25.00.** *Courtesy Robin Englehart, vintagelane.com, photo by Nancy Jean Mong.*

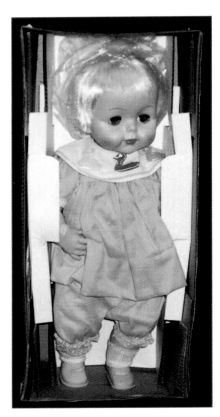

Tickles: 20" battery-operated doll cries when you spank her and laughs when you tickle her. Tickles is marked "19©63/DELUXE READING CORP./75." MIB: **$75.00 – 100.00.** *Courtesy Michele Casino.*

Baby Boo: Deluxe Reading's 19" battery-operated Baby Boo doll has a crying mechanism inside her torso. Baby Boo originally came with a pacifier that when pulled out the doll cried. When the pacifier was placed back in her mouth she stopped crying. She also cried when she was placed close to a light and stopped when removed from the light. The doll in the photo is wearing the original dress to Deluxe Reading's Tickles doll. Baby Boo is marked "E326/DELUXE READING CORP./©1965" on her head. On the back of her battery cover she is marked "CAT.NO 1613 ©D.L.R. CORP. 1965/MADE BY/DELUXE READING CORPORATION/ELIZABETHPORT, NEW JERSEY/U.S. OF AMERICA PAT. APPLIED FOR" along with "REMOVE THESE SCREWS/TO REPLACE BATTERIES." Re-dressed/working: **$35.00 – 55.00.**

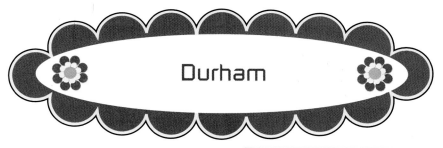

Durham

Skinny Jimmy and Skinny Jinny: 11" flat vinyl dolls. The dolls are marked with a picture of the world and the letter "I" inside a "D"/No 1500/Durham Industries, Inc./New York, NY 10010/Made in Taiwan." The year of these dolls is unknown. MIB: **$20.00 – 25.00 each.** *Courtesy Robin Englehart, vintagelane.com, photo by Nancy Jean Mong.*

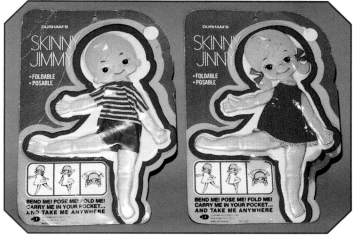

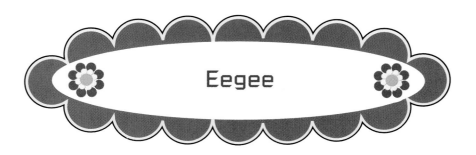

L'il Sister: 9½" doll similar to Mattel's Skipper doll. MIB: **$35.00 – 45.00.** *Courtesy Rebecca Wingler.*

Miss Sunbeam: 17¾" Miss Sunbeam in her original box. The same box was used for another doll named Karen as there is a Miss Sunbeam sticker placed over the other doll's name. **$45.00 – 50.00.** *Courtesy Ann Wagner.*

Miss Sunbeam: Two 17¾" Miss Sunbeam dolls. Both are marked "Eegee" on the back of their heads, and unmarked on their bodies. The doll on the left has a hard plastic torso and limbs and a rigid vinyl head. The doll on the right has hard plastic legs and torso and vinyl head and arms. **$25.00 – 35.00 each.** *Courtesy Ann Wagner.*

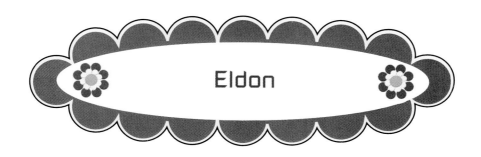

Eldon

Baby Joy's Tiny Room: This playset came in a 15⅜" x 13" x 6½" plastic case with a carrying handle. The furniture in the room is attached to the floor. The room includes a crib, a playpen, a dresser, a highchair, and a changing table. The doll in the playset is just under 4" and is marked "ELDON/JAPAN" on her back. The sticker on the case reads "Baby Joy's™ Tinyroom™. Take it anywhere — use it with any 4" doll." and "ELDON®/Just for the fun of it. ©1966Eldon Industries, Inc., Hawthorne, California/Printed in U.S.A. Pat. Pending Part No. 5-15-307." and " * Nothing else to buy. * Complete with doll, clothes, permanent plastic furniture with movable parts — duck, feeding dish, and bottle. * Carrying case with removable lid. Stock No. 9820." Eldon also sold a similar playset called Sandy's Tiny Room which featured a "swingin'" teen doll in a "mod" recreation/bedroom. **$60.00 – 75.00.**

Pipsqueeks: 5" tall fun play people from 1970. The Pipsqueeks included a stewardess, a pilot, a fire chief, and a doctor. The figures' heads squeak and they talk "pipsqueek" language. Shown in the photo is the stewardess. NRFP: **$20.00 – 25.00.** *Courtesy Michele Casino.*

Fisher-Price

Natalie: This doll is one of Fisher-Price's lapsitters from 1973. Natalie is 14" with a stuffed body, stuffed legs and arms, a vinyl head, and vinyl hands. Other dolls in the line include Elizabeth, Mary, Audrey, Jenny, Baby Ann, and Joey. Each doll, in addition to being marked on his/her head, has a Fisher Price tag on his/her body that gives information about the company, where the doll was assembled, material content, and a number which is probably the catalog or style number that identifies the doll. MIB: **$50.00 – 75.00.**

Fisher-Price's Lapsitters: Back of Natalie's box showing six of the seven lapsitter dolls. Joey is not shown in the photo as he was issued the following year.

Susie Sad Eyes: It is believed this doll was used by several companies including Fun-World. A small following of collectors feel that the Susie Sad Eyes dolls were inspired by the work of artist Margret Keane who was famous for her big-eyed children portraits, which were especially popular in the 1960s. Because of interest in these dolls by Keane collectors, values for them have risen in recent years, even though the doll is relatively common and not the best quality. 8" Susie Sad Eyes is marked "L. (bell shaped design) B./915/66 A/MADE IN HONG KONG" on her head and "MADE IN HONG KONG" on her back. In original clothing: **$15.00 – 25.00.** *Courtesy Robin Englehart, vintage lane.com, photo by Nancy Jean Mong.*

Susie Slicker: Susie Slicker was basically the same doll as Susie Sad Eyes, only she came dressed in a vinyl raincoat, hat (missing in photo), and boots. Susie Slicker was issued by Fun-World. MIB: **$25.00 – 35.00.** *Courtesy Robin Englehart, vintagelane.com, photo by Nancy Jean Mong.*

Lil' Disco Doll: 6" doll similar to Topper's Dawn doll. Her box reads, "#8612 ©Fun-World, Div. Glen Cove, NY. 11542/Made in Hong Kong." NRFC: **$25.00 – 30.00.**

Kitty Coed: 6" doll. Box reads, "Another/Huggles/by Fun World." Kitty Coed dolls came with different hair colors and styles and different outfits. MIB: **$20.00 – 25.00.** *Courtesy Robin Englehart, vintagelane.com, photo by Nancy Jean Mong.*

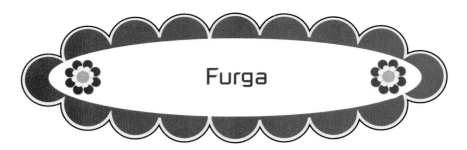

Furga

Many of the Furga dolls pictured here were advertised in only one of the major department store catalogs, instead of several different ones as most dolls usually were. It is unknown if Furga often sold specific dolls exclusively to one major store, yet if they did, the dolls were not advertised in those store's catalogs as being store exclusives. It is probable these dolls were also available at other stores in addition to the ones listed here.

Damina: This doll was shown in the 1966 Sears Christmas catalog. The 14" doll is marked "Furga Italy" on the back of her neck. MIB: **$135.00 – 150.00.** *Courtesy Karen Edland.*

Guendalina: Guendalina was shown in the 1966 Sears Christmas catalog. The 14" doll is marked "Furga Italy" on the back of her neck. MIB: **$135.00 – 150.00.** *Courtesy Karen Edland.*

Crown Princess/Elisabetta: This doll was sold under the name Crown Princess in Montgomery Wards Christmas catalogs from 1967 to 1969, but was then listed as Elisabetta in Montgomery Wards 1970 – 1974 Christmas catalogs. The 14" doll is marked "Furga Italy" on the back of her neck. Although easier to find than many of the other Furga dolls shown here, her value is comparable to the other harder-to-find dolls since she tends to be popular with collectors. MIB: **$135.00 – 150.00.** *Courtesy Karen Edland.*

Gabriella: Gabriella was shown in the 1969 Montgomery Wards Christmas catalog. The 18" doll is marked "Furga Italy" on the back of her neck. MIB: **$135.00 – 150.00.** *Courtesy Karen Edland.*

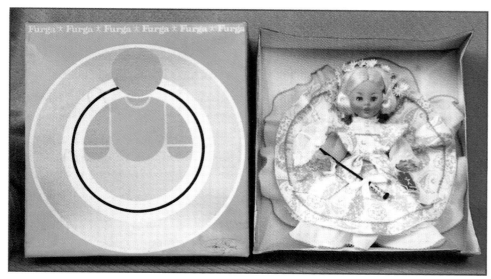

Cristina: Shown in the 1969 J.C. Penney Christmas catalog. The 15" doll is marked "Furga Italy" on the back of her neck. MIB: **$135.00 – 150.00.** *Courtesy Karen Edland.*

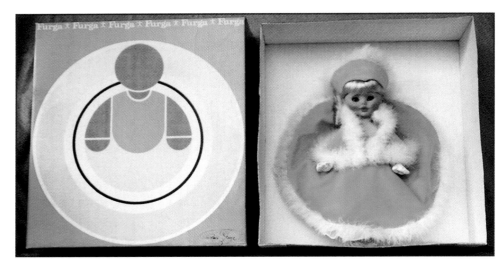

Angela: This doll was shown in the 1970 Sears Christmas catalog. The 14" doll is marked "Furga Itay" on the back of her neck. MIB: **$125.00 – 145.00.** *Courtesy Karen Edland.*

Raffaella: 23" doll marked "Furga Italy" on the back of her neck. Year sold is unknown. MIB: **$125.00.** *Courtesy Karen Edland.*

Fiorenza: Fiorenza was shown in the 1971 – 1973 Montgomery Wards Christmas catalogs. The 18" doll is marked "Furga Italy" on the back of her neck. MIB: **$95.00 – 125.00.** *Courtesy Karen Edland.*

Vittoria and Valentina: The blond doll in the blue outfit is Valentina and the brunette doll in red is Vittoria. The 15" vinyl dolls have poseable vinyl legs and arms and a twist waist. Their original box opens up into a couch. These dolls were shown in the 1969 and 1970 Sears Christmas catalog. MIB: **$50.00 – 65.00.** *Courtesy Karen Hickey.*

Tina and Tilly: These 7" dolls came in a variety of hair colors, styles, and outfits. The dolls' original box doesn't indicate which doll is inside but using the 1970 Sears Christmas catalog as a guide it appears the dolls with bangs are Tilly and the dolls with side or center parted hair are Tina. MIB: **$30.00 – 40.00.** Loose: **$10.00 – 20.00.** *Courtesy Karen Hickey.*

FASHION DOLLS
"Mommy, these must be the

Two 15-inch Italian Beauties with skin that feels like real .. waists that twist 'n turn .. and limbs that pose any way you want them to

Valentina

Vittoria

Each $6.99

Spirited, stylish and beautiful—they've captured the look of today! With gently curved arms and shapely legs .. bright, clear eyes shining from beneath their long, long lashes .. and silky, rooted hair you can comb and style again and again. Made by Furga of a new, supple vinyl that's softer, more bendable than ever before. Dressed in mini wrap-arounds fastened with an initial pin; sandals.
49 C 30369—Brown-haired Vittoria. Shipping weight 1 pound 8 ounces................$6.99
49 C 30368—Blonde Valentina. Shipping weight 1 pound 8 ounces.....................6.99

Italian-inspired Outfits ..
designed to turn Vittoria and Valentina into the prettiest swingers to hit any scene

1 Elegant blue velvet evening dress with organdy ruffles on collar, sleeves, hem. Gold-color chain belt and sandals.
49 C 30642—Shpg. wt. 8 oz..........$6.99

2 Leather-look vinyl coat has plush orange pile front lining, matching hat. Boots.
49 C 30639—Shpg. wt. 8 oz..........$5.99

3 Lounging pajamas in a pretty cotton print with contrasting band trim. Sandals.
49 C 30637—Shpg. wt. 8 oz..........$4.99

4 Delicious apricot velvet evening pants and tunic with long sleeves edged in marabou, gold-color chain belt. Sandals.
49 C 30641—Shpg. wt. 8 oz..........$6.99

5 Perky linen dress has a painted daisy .. contrasting collar, cuffs. Boots, purse.
49 C 30638—Shpg. wt. 8 oz..........$3.99

Note: Dolls not included with items 1 through 5.

Vittoria and Valentina: 1969 Sears Christmas catalog showing some of the fashions available for Vittoria and Valentina.

family name . . dolls of such realism, grace and loveliness they'll be treasured a lifetime. When you're thinking of the most beautiful dolls in the world—think **Furga** ✕

$6⁹⁹ each

☐1 Vittoria

☐2 Valentina

Italian Ensembles for Vittoria and Valentina

3 Bright little mini with lace-up boots, purse. Wt. 7 oz.
49 N 32524 . . . . $3.99

4 Sensational . . full length gown and elegant wrap with soft marabou trim. Gold-color evening slippers, too. Shpg. wt. 8 oz.
49 N 32523 . . . . $6.99

5 Mod bell-bottom pants with vest, shirt and matching scarf. Snap moc-toe shoes.
49 N 32522—Wt. 8 oz . . $5.99

6 Perky lace-trimmed dress with daisy applique. Shoes.
49 N 32525—Wt. 7 oz . . $4.99

7 Stunning fur-trimmed maxi-coat with matching hat and long boots.
49 N 32521—Wt. 9 oz . . $5.99

NOTE: Dolls not included with outfits above.

SO BENDABLE . . so you can rotate, tilt, twist and turn them . . so lifelike even their skin feels real.

Completely poseable 15-inch Italian lovelies

Spirited, stylish and oh, so poseable . . no wonder these Italian beauties are such favorites. Both dolls have gently curved arms, shapely legs and bright, clear eyes shining from beneath their long, long lashes. Their silky rooted hair can be combed and styled again and again. Made by Furga of a supple vinyl that's incredibly soft and bendable. They're wearing mini wrap-arounds and sandals.
(1) 49 N 30369—Brownette Vittoria. Shipping weight 1 pound 8 ounces $6.99
(2) 49 N 30368—Blonde Valentina. Shipping weight 1 pound 8 ounces 6.99

Poseable 7-inch Tina and Tilly

They love wearing their Furga-designed outfits $2⁹⁹ each

Soft vinyl Italian cuties with shiny rooted hair and bright go-to-sleep eyes. Shoes incl.

8 Blonde Tina in sporty slacks and blouse.
49 N 37007—Shpg. wt. 7 oz. $2.99

9 Brunette Tina with snappy coat and cap.
49 N 37006—Shpg. wt. 7 oz. $2.99

10 Brunette Tilly in perky dress.
49 N 37012—Shpg. wt. 7 oz. $2.99

11 Blonde Tina in swingin' slacks and topper.
49 N 37005—Shpg. wt. 7 oz. $2.99

12 Orange-haired Tilly in slacks and sweater.
49 N 37008—Shpg. wt. 7 oz. $2.99

13 Blonde Tilly in a mod jumpsuit.
49 N 37011—Shpg. wt. 7 oz. $2.99

PCBKM   Sears 601

Vittoria and Valentina, Tina and Tilly: 1970 Sears Christmas catalog showing more fashions available for Vittoria and Valentina, as well as Tina and Tilly.

Virna: 18" doll marked "Furga Italy" on the back of her neck. Year sold is unknown. MIB: **$75.00 – 100.00.** *Courtesy Karen Edland.*

Elena: 14" doll marked "Furga Italy" on the back of her neck. Year sold is unknown. MIB: **$75.00 – 100.00.** *Courtesy Karen Edland.*

As dolls made with pride in exquisite gowns, these breathtaking belles are the toast of the town...

DOLLS by FURGA of ITALY

Beautiful Bride from Italy $9.99

Brunette beauty attends her bridal ball in a gown of white lace and velveteen-type fabric. Short lace-trimmed veil. Fully jointed doll has vinyl skin, rooted hair, movable blue eyes. White lingerie, socks, shoes. 12 in. tall. Ages 5 and up.

Wt. 1 lb. 3 oz.

49 N 32049............$9.99

● REMEMBER!
You can order items on pages 425 to 593 from now until AUGUST 15, 1975

(1 thru 5) Our finest dolls .. so finely crafted, even their shiny rooted hair is arranged by hand. They have creamy vinyl skin, classic features and sparkling blue movable eyes with long lashes. Sensationally lavish gowns. Frilly lingerie, shoes and posing stand included with each doll. For ages 5 and up.

1 15-inch **Arianna.** Gorgeous green felt gown with white ruffled undergown. Matching green felt hat. Shpg. wt. 3 lbs.
79 N 32081C............$18.99

2 15-inch **Alina.** Dainty dress of red, white and blue, check-pattern batiste material. White organdie blouse, hat. Shipping weight 3 pounds.
79 N 32082C............$24.99

3 18-inch **Milena.** Rich orange gown and hat of synthetic velvet. White accent. Parasol.
79 N 32065C—Shpg. wt. 4 lbs............$34.99

4 18-inch **Miriam.** Sensational white lace and pink taffeta ensemble. Dress trimmed with pink "roses". Matching lace-trimmed hat.
79 N 32093C—Shpg. wt. 4 lbs............$29.99

5 18-inch **Marina.** Fancy frock of white laced fabric, taffeta undergown. Light blue apron.
79 N 32083C—Shpg. wt. 3 lbs............$29.99

432 Sears

Furga Dolls: Sears 1974 Christmas catalog showing some of the Furga dolls available that year.

Emerald the Enchanting Witch: Back of Emerald's original box. *Courtesy Joyce McCandless.*

Emerald the Enchanting Witch: A loose Emerald the Enchanting Witch wearing her original outfit. All original: **$55.00 – 75.00.** *Courtesy Lisa Petrucci.*

Emerald the Enchanting Witch: Purple 6½" battery-operated doll with green hair and green eyes that light up. Emerald originally came dressed in a black shiny vinyl playsuit, witch's hat, and black vinyl boots. She had several additional outfits that could be purchased separately. Emerald is marked "©/1972/GIRLS/WORLD/PAT.PEND./ MADE/IN/JAPAN" on the back of her removable battery cover. MIB: **$150.00 – 300.00.** *Courtesy Lisa Petrucci.*

Emerald the Enchanting Witch: This photo shows a loose Emerald doll wearing her nightgown, a NRFB Emerald doll, and a loose Emerald wearing her original outfit. Loose dolls with original outfit or Emerald outfit sold separately: **$55.00 – 75.00.** MIB: **$150.00 – 300.00.** *Courtesy Lisa Petrucci.*

Emerald the Enchanting Witch: Emerald outfit Bewitched. NRFP: **$65.00 – 100.00.** *Courtesy Joyce McCandless.*

Emerald the Enchanting Witch: Emerald outfit Midnight Ride. NRFP: **$45.00 – 75.00.** *Courtesy Joyce McCandless.*

Emerald the Enchanting Witch: Emerald outfit Morning Mist. NRFP: **$45.00 – 75.00.** *Courtesy Joyce McCandless.*

Emerald the Enchanting Witch: Emerald outfit Nightgown. NRFP: **$40.00 – 50.00.** *Courtesy Joyce McCandless.*

Emerald the Enchanting Witch: Emerald outfit Saucy Sprite. NRFP: **$45.00 – 75.00.** *Courtesy Joyce McCandless.*

Emerald the Enchanting Witch: Emerald shown with her hard-to-find house which was sold separately. House: **$100.00 – 165.00.** *Courtesy Michele Casino.*

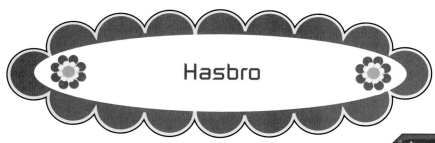

Hasbro

Little Miss No Name: 15" Little Miss No Name originally came dressed in a burlap dress and had a teardrop falling from her eye. The doll is made of a lightweight plastic that easily broke and her hair tended to become dry and fall out over time so finding a doll in good condition isn't always easy. It is common to find the teardrop missing from loose dolls, so when present it adds to the value of the doll. Many adults remember this doll from their childhoods, so consequently she is popular with collectors today. Value for loose dolls varies quite a bit depending on if she is wearing her original dress and the condition of the doll. She is easily found but hard to find in mint condition. Little Miss No Name is marked on her head "©1965 HASBRO®." All original with box: **$200.00 – 275.00.** Loose dolls, all original: **$30.00 – 85.00.** *Courtesy Michele Casino.*

Peteena: 9" doll with head of a poodle and body of a doll. Here she is shown in her original box. Peteena is marked "©1966/HASBRO®/JAPAN/PATENT PENDING" on her back. MIB: **$85.00 – 125.00.** *Courtesy Robin Englehart, vintagelane.com, photo by Nancy Jean Mong.*

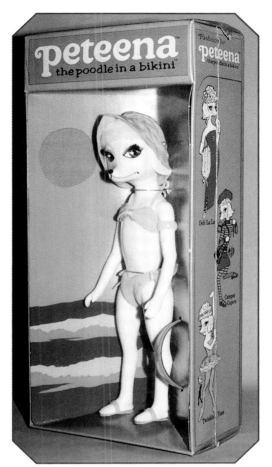

Peteena: Back of Peteena's original box. *Courtesy Robin Englehart, vintagelane.com, photo by Nancy Jean Mong.*

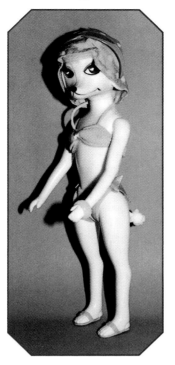

Peteena: Peteena wearing her original outfit. This outfit was called Surf's Up and included a two-piece bikini, hat, bracelet, sunglasses, and yellow sandals. The tail of the doll often comes off so if it is missing, value is lowered considerably. Loose with tail and original outfit: **$50.00 – 65.00.** *Courtesy Robin Englehart, vintagelane.com, photo by Nancy Jean Mong.*

Peteena: Peteena in her original box shown with three other dolls wearing outfits sold separately for her. Some pieces of Peteena's clothing are tagged, "Peteena™/ BY HASBRO®/JAPAN." All Peteena's outfits are hard to find. Loose outfits mint and complete without dolls: **$35.00 – 70.00.** *Courtesy Robin Englehart, vintagelane.com, photo by Nancy Jean Mong.*

Peteena: Peteena wearing her Slicker Set (#9011) rain outfit. Slicker Set includes a black and yellow vinyl rain slicker with matching black rain hat, a yellow and black tasseled-handle umbrella, yellow and black striped rain boots, and a yellow vinyl bag (pictured below). Outfit only: **$35.00 – 55.00.** *Courtesy Robin Englehart, vintagelane.com, photo by Nancy Jean Mong.*

Peteena: Peteena in her Zero Cool (#9012) ski outfit which includes a one-piece turtleneck bodysuit, a zippered sweater, skis, ski poles, goggles, black boots, matching fur mittens and hat. Outfit only: **$45.00 – 55.00.** *Courtesy Robin Englehart, vintagelane.com, photo by Nancy Jean Mong.*

Peteena: Peteena wearing her Twinkle Toes (#9015) ballerina costume. The outfit includes a pink velveteen tutu edged with lace and trimmed with velveteen flowers, pink tights, a floral headpiece, blue vinyl ballet slippers with ribbon lacings, a black stretch rehearsal leotard, and black tights. Outfit only: **$30.00 – 55.00.** *Courtesy Robin Englehart, vintagelane.com, photo by Nancy Jean Mong.*

Peteena: Peteena models her outfit Campus Capers. The outfit consists of a blue and burgundy striped pullover shirt with a burgundy elastic belt (often missing), matching striped knit tights, a burgundy knit beret, burgundy vinyl Mary Jane shoes, a black vinyl purse, an orange megaphone, orange "STATE" pennant with fringe, black vinyl book strap holding three books: *Alice in Wonderland, World Atlas,* and *Care and Feeding of Dogs.* Outfit only: **$40.00 – 70.00.** *Courtesy Robin Englehart, vintagelane.com, photo by Nancy Jean Mong.*

Peteena: Peteena wearing her outfit Ooh La La. This outfit includes a rose satin evening gown with a pearl cluster on the bodice, a satin stole trimmed with white fur, long white evening gloves, vinyl evening flats with gold accents on the front, sheer beige stockings, a gold vinyl clutch with a pearl closure, a pearl choker with two pink pearl accents, and pearl drop earrings. Outfit only: **$35.00 – 65.00.** *Courtesy Robin Englehart, vintagelane.com, photo by Nancy Jean Mong.*

Peteena T.M.

TV's newest collector doll sensation!

A new concept in dolls...a Paris inspired fashion poodle that will sell like the Paris originals!

Every now and then a fantastic new item comes along. Imaginative! Daring! Almost shocking! Yet you know it will be a sensation. Peteena is that kind of item! She's a sophisticated creation that is in step with the times . . . in tune with today's active younger generation. They will take to her because she is what she is . . . unusual, different, provocative! And television will introduce and sell Peteena to the millions of youngsters waiting to buy her. Get enough of her today . . . because she'll be the hottest thing in the toy business tomorrow!

Peteena: Page from Hasbro dealer catalog showing Peteena wearing her fashions. *Courtesy Stephanie Strait.*

Flying Nun: In 1967 Hasbro acquired a license to manufacture many Flying Nun toys including dolls made in the image of Sally Fields who played the part of Sister Bertrille on the *Flying Nun* television series. In the photo is Hasbro's 11½" Flying Nun doll shown in her original box. The doll bares some similarities to Horsman's 11" Mary Poppins and Patty Duke dolls. MIB: **$150.00 – 225.00.** *Courtesy Kathleen Tornikoski, Romancing the Doll.*

Dolly Darlings: 4" Dolly Darling dolls either had molded hair or rooted hair. The molded hair doll shown here is Beth at the Supermarket. She came packaged inside a round plastic hatbox case and came with a number of small accessories mounted on a cardboard backing inside the hatbox. Beth is marked "©1965/HASBRO®/JAPAN" on her back. In case with never-removed accessories: **$45.00 – 65.00.** *Courtesy Karen Hickey.*

Dolly Darlings Play Room: Four different play rooms were issued for Dolly Darlings. They included a living room, bedroom, bathroom, and kitchen. The rooms had a removable plastic cover and came with a Dolly Darlings doll. Shown is Slumber Party in the Dolly Darlings' bathroom. **$50.00 – 85.00.** *Courtesy Karen Hickey.*

Flower Darlings: Hasbro's Flower Darlings were 3½" dolls which stood inside plastic flower pins. The Flower Darlings include Daisy, Dahlia, Daphne, Lily, Rose, and Violet. The dolls are marked "©1968/HASBRO®/HONG KONG" on their backs. The photo shows Rose Darling inside her original package. NRFP: **$35.00 – 45.00 each.**

Storykins: In 1969, Hasbro created these 2" – 3½" tiny dolls. There were nine different Storykins sets including Mother Hubbard, Goldilocks, Cinderella, Prince Charming, Sleeping Beauty, Snow White, The Jungle Book, Rumpelstiltskin, and Pinocchio. The dolls and their accessories originally came packaged inside a plastic bubble mounted on a cardboard backing. A small-sized 33⅓ rpm record was included with each set. The dolls are marked "©1967/HASBRO/HONG KONG" on their backs. Values for loose Storykins are determined by rarity and completeness of set, as well as flaws such as discoloration of vinyl and in the case of the larger sized dolls if they still pose. Cinderella, Goldilocks, and Sleeping Beauty are by far the easiest Storykins to find. Loose, complete sets of these three dolls can be found for under $20.00 each. Slightly harder to find are Mother Hubbard, Rumpelstiltskin, and Prince Charming. Storykins Snow White is difficult to find, especially in a complete set with the dwarves. Pinocchio and The Jungle Book sets are the hardest Storykins to find. Shown in the photo is Rumpelstiltskin in his original package. NRFP: **$75.00 – 95.00.** *Courtesy Robin Englehart, vintagelane.com, photo by Nancy Jean Mong.*

Storykins: Loose Rumpelstiltskin with his spinning wheel. Loose and complete: **$35.00 – 45.00.**

Storykins: This Storykins Cinderella doll was a mail-away premium. Cinderella was also sold in stores in a carded package like the one Rumpelstilskin is shown in above. Loose Cinderella Storykins are fairly easy to find, but when loose she is often missing her clear vinyl shoes or the crown on her head (not seen in photo). Both of these items add to her value. Mint/complete with mail-away box: **$25.00 – 35.00.** *Courtesy Robin Englehart, vintagelane.com, photo by Nancy Jean Mong.*

World of Love Dolls: In 1971 Hasbro issued their World of Love line of dolls. Sporting mod names like Love, Peace, Soul, and Flower, the World of Love dolls were hip with the times. The female dolls in the line had long rooted eyelashes and bendable legs. These two photos show a 1972 Love doll which came in a deluxe set that featured a doll and extra outfit. The doll in the deluxe set (left) had brighter blond hair then the standard Love doll and came dressed in a green shirt with her name on the front and matching green panties. Her extra outfit (right) was a yellow nylon midi-dress with a floral cotton overdress. The 9" doll is marked "MADE IN/HONG KONG" on her back and "©HASBRO/U.S.PAT PEND" on her lower body. Loose wearing Love fashions: **$15.00 – 20.00.** *Courtesy Robin Englehart, vintagelane.com, photo by Nancy Jean Mong.*

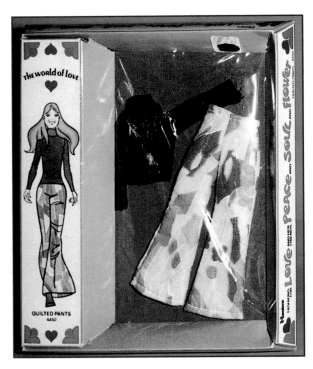

World of Love Dolls: World of Love Fashion #4450 Quilted Pants. NRFP: **$20.00 – 25.00.** *Courtesy Robin Englehart, vintagelane.com, photo by Nancy Jean Mong.*

World of Love Dolls: World of Love Fashion #4452 Belted Jumpsuit. NRFP: **$20.00 – 25.00.** *Courtesy Robin Englehart, vintagelane.com, photo by Nancy Jean Mong.*

World of Love Dolls: World of Love Fashion #4454 Sport Gear. NRFP: **$20.00 – 25.00.** *Courtesy Robin Englehart, vintagelane.com, photo by Nancy Jean Mong.*

World of Love Dolls: World of Love Fashion #4455 Multi-Color Mini. NRFP: **$20.00 – 25.00.** *Courtesy Robin Englehart, vintagelane.com, photo by Nancy Jean Mong.*

World of Love Dolls: World of Love Fashion #4471 Jazzy Jeans. NRFP: **$20.00 – 25.00.** *Courtesy Robin Englehart, vintagelane.com, photo by Nancy Jean Mong.*

World of Love Dolls: Back of the World of Love Fashion box showing illustrations of the groovy dolls in the line. *Courtesy Robin Englehart, vintagelane.com, photo by Nancy Jean Mong.*

Leggy: Hasbro's 10" Leggy dolls were named for the exaggerated length of their legs. The dolls in the line included Jill, Kate, Nan, and Sue. They came dressed in brightly colored mod clothes like bell bottoms, halter tops, and platform shoes. In addition, they had many outfits sold separately for them. In Europe, Leggy dolls were marketed by Polistil under license by Hasbro. The European dolls were the same as the U.S. dolls, but went by numbers instead of names. Shown in the photo is the European equivalent to Leggy Nan, who had the stock number LG2. Both American and European Leggy dolls are marked "©1972®/HASBRO/HONG KONG" on their lower bodies. NRFP: **$45.00 – 75.00.** *Courtesy Robin Englehart, vintagelane.com, photo by Nancy Jean Mong.*

Flutter-byes: 1½" dolls that came with rooted pink, orange, blue, yellow, or green hair. They had removable plastic wings. NRFP: **$20.00 – 25.00.** *Courtesy Robin Englehart, vintagelane.com, photo by Nancy Jean Mong.*

Flutter-byes: Orange-haired Flutter-bye. The doll is marked "HASBRO IND./©1973" on her head. **$5.00 – 10.00.**

Horsman

Mary Poppins: Horsman's popular 11½" Mary Poppins doll delighted youngsters for many years. The doll was first issued in 1963 and was still available into the early 1970s. Because the doll was issued for so long, today it is relatively easy to find. A Mary Poppins doll in played with condition without the original box and complete outfit is worth about **$10.00 – 20.00.** If she has her complete outfit, value can go up to **$25.00 – 45.00,** depending on the condition of the doll and outfit. Mint in box values vary depending on the set. The Mary Poppins doll shown in the photo was made for Horsman's 50th anniversary. The doll came with a paper umbrella, but other versions of Mary Poppins came with a vinyl umbrella that opened and closed. Mary Poppins is marked "H" on her head. MIB: **$55.00 – 75.00.**

Mary Poppins: Close-up of the same MIB Mary Poppins doll.

Mary Poppins, Jane, and Michael: These dolls representing the characters from the Walt Disney movie *Mary Poppins* were available in a set with all three dolls or Jane and Michael could be purchased in a set without the Mary Poppins doll. 8" Michael is marked "©3(digit varies)/HORSMAN DOLLS INC./6682" on his head. 8" Jane is marked "©7(digit varies)/HORSMAN DOLLS INC./6681" on her head. Mary Poppins is marked "H" on her head. Although Mary Poppins is the easiest doll to find of the three, more collectors seem to want her so her value is about the same as the harder-to-find children. Loose dolls in original clothing in slightly played with condition: **$25.00 – 40.00 each.** *Courtesy Ann Wagner.*

Mary Poppins: These three photos show Horsman's 11½" Mary Poppins dolls in the different outfits she was sold with. Mint/loose doll in complete original outfit: **$35.00 – 40.00.** *Courtesy Robin Englehart, vintagelane.com, photo by Nancy Jean Mong.*

Patty Duke: This doll represents teenage actress Patty Duke when she was starring in the *Patty Duke Show* on television. The 11" tall doll is marked "H" on her head. **$100.00 – 125.00.**

Thirstee Walker: From around 1963 and continuing throughout the 1960s, Horsman used the Thirstee Walker name or some variation of it for many of their dolls. In addition to Thirstee Walker, there was Drinkee Walker, Mini Thirstee Strutter, Life-size Thirstee Baby, Thirstee Cry Baby, Drinkee Baby, and Mini Thirstee Baby. Many of these dolls came in different sizes. In addition, Horsman used the Thirsty Walker face mold for several other dolls. Often people generically call any large Horsman walking doll with cupped hands a Thirstee Walker doll, but in actuality it may have been a Drinkee Walker or even a My Baby and Me doll, which like many Thirstee Walker dolls was 27", but came clutching a small doll in her cupped hands instead of a baby bottle. Without the original box or original clothing it is hard to tell if a doll is actually one of the Thirstee line or another Horsman doll that used the Thirstee face mold. The doll in the photo is a re-dressed doll made with the Thirstee Walker mold. Without her original clothes it's difficult to determine if she is definitely Thirstee Walker. She is 27" and is marked "HORSMAN DOLLS, INC./19©64/TB25" on her neck. Re-dressed doll: **$25.00 – 30.00.**

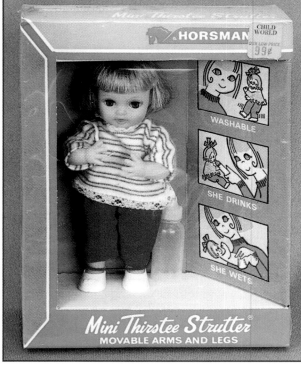

Life-size Thirstee Baby: 17" Life-size Thirstee Baby has a large open mouth to hold a baby bottle. Other dolls in various sizes were made with the Thirstee Baby mold including Thirstee Cry Baby (battery operated), Drinkee Baby, Baby Buttercup, and some versions of Baby Kicks. When these dolls are loose and their true identity is unknown, they are generically referred to as Thirstee Baby by collectors. Thirstee Baby came in various hair colors, has a vinyl head and limbs, and a plastic body. Her blue eyes open and close. She is marked "©HORSMAN DOLLS, INC." on her neck. The doll in the photo has been re-dressed. Re-dressed doll: **$15.00 – 20.00.**

Mini Thirstee Strutter: A miniature version of Thirstee Walker. The 6½" vinyl doll has open and shut eyes, and like the larger dolls comes with her own baby bottle. A Mini Thirstee Baby was made using this same face mold. NRFB: **$20.00 – 25.00.**

Heavenly Baby: The two Zodiac dolls on the right called Heavenly Baby have the same face as Horsman's Mini Thirstee Strutter shown on the left. Mini Thirstee Strutter is 6½" and the two Heavenly Babies are 6". The Heavenly Baby dolls came with charm bracelets with all 12 signs of the Zodiac on the six coin charms. All three dolls are marked on their heads, "Horsman Dolls Inc./19©68." **$15.00 – 25.00 each.** *Courtesy Ann Wagner.*

Gloria Jean: 15½" doll with vinyl head and arms and hard plastic torso and legs. She has two-tone frosted hair and blue sleep eyes. She is marked "1963 Irene Szor/Horsman Dolls Inc." on her head. The dress she is wearing is original but the same doll was sold in several different outfits as well. **$35.00 – 45.00.** *Courtesy Ann Wagner.*

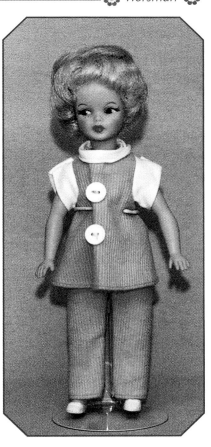

Peggy: This 9½" doll strongly resembles Ideal's Pepper doll. Peggy is marked "Horsman/©64/900" on her neck. She is wearing just one of many outfits she originally came dressed in. **$10.00 – 15.00.** *Courtesy Sally Seikel.*

Peggy: Horsman's Peggy doll wearing another one of her original outfits. **$10.00 – 15.00.** *Courtesy Rebecca Wingler, photo by Paul Magann.*

Lullaby Baby: 12" doll wiggles while the music box inside her plays Brahms' Lullaby. Lullaby Baby has inset plastic eyes, and six speaker holes cut in the vinyl on her stomach. She came dressed in a variety of different outfits. She is marked "2/HORSMAN DOLLS INC./19©67" on her head. The doll in the photo has been re-dressed. Re-dressed and working: **$20.00 – 25.00.**

69

The Pip Squeaks: 13" vinyl dolls with squeakers in their arms. The dolls included Cleo, Mark, Anthony, and Patty. The dolls are marked "Horsman Dolls, Inc./1967/0712-A." Sears 1967 Christmas Catalog. **$15.00 – 25.00 each.**

Perfume Pixies: 3" scented doll similar to Mattel's Kologne Kiddles. They were available starting in 1968. Loose dolls without their perfume bottle containers are only worth **$2.00 – 3.00 each,** but with bottle and tag, are in the **$10.00 – 15.00** range. **$10.00 – 15.00.** *Courtesy Robin Englehart, vintagelane.com, photo by Nancy Jean Mong.*

Tessie Talk: 17" ventriloquist doll has two holes in the back of her head where strings come through. When the strings are pulled her mouth opens and closes as if she were talking. Tessie is marked "HORSMAN DOLL INC./19©74" on her head and "HORSMAN DOLL INC." on her back. **$25.00 – 35.00.** *Courtesy Robin Englehart, vintagelane.com, photo by Nancy Jean Mong.*

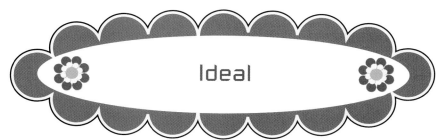

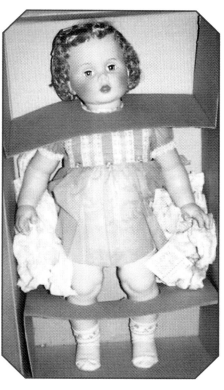

Penny Playpal: This 32" doll is Patti Playpal's two-year old sister. She was only available in 1959. Penny Playpal came with curly hair in varying lengths and was issued in both blond and brunette. She is marked "IDEAL TOY CO./32-E-L" on her head and "IDEAL" on her back. MIB: **$500.00 – 625.00.** *Courtesy Hillary and Cliff James, Toy With Me.*

Patite: 18" doll looks like a miniature version of Patty Playpal. She was available in 1960 – 1961. Patite is marked "©/IDEAL TOY CORP/G18" on her head and back. This doll is hard to find and very popular with collectors because of her similarity to Patti Playpal. The doll in the photo has been re-dressed in a replica outfit. Re-dressed: **$250.00 – 350.00.** *Courtesy Ann Wagner.*

Miss Ideal/Terry Twist: This 1961 doll came in a 25" size, like the one shown here, as well as in a 30" size. Miss Ideal was issued in 1961 and came in various hair colors and styles. She was available in many different outfits including the capri-styled outfit she is wearing in the photo. The doll has a swivel waist and jointed ankles. In 1962 Miss Ideal was called Terry Twist. Miss Ideal is marked "©IDEAL TOY CORP./SP-25-6" on her head and "©IDEAL TOY CORP./P-25" on her back. **$275.00 – 325.00.**

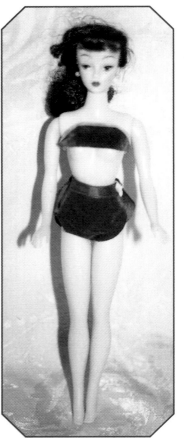

Mitzi: In 1961 Ideal sold their "modern teenage doll" Mitzi who was 11¼" size and looked quite a bit like Mattel's Barbie doll. The doll in the photo is shown wearing her original outfit. Mitzi is marked "MITZI/©IDEAL TOY CORP./ MCMLX/2" on her back. Loose doll with original outfit: **$40.00 – 55.00.** *Courtesy Ann Wagner.*

Mitzi: Her markings are slightly different than the doll shown on the left, "MITZI/©IDEAL TOY CORP./MCMLX/1" on her back. The doll in the photo has been re-dressed. Loose doll, re-dressed: **$25.00 – 35.00.**

Tiny Thumbelina (14") and Thumbelina (20"): So many collectors remember the doll Thumbelina from their childhood. There were a whole variety of Thumbelina dolls produced in the 1960s and 1970s, but the most popular ones with collectors today are the Thumbelina dolls with the windup knobs on their back. Available in several different sizes, Thumbelina looks like a newborn baby and when her wind-up knob is turned she squirms and wiggles like a newborn. She has a plush body and vinyl head and limbs. The hair on these Thumbelina dolls didn't hold up well over the years so finding a doll with a full head of hair is a big challenge for collectors. The 14" Tiny Thumbelina doll shown here is marked "©IDEAL TOY CORP./OTT-14." The 20" Thumbelina in the photo has a wooden wind-up knob and is marked "©IDEAL TOY CORP./OTT-19" on her head. Both dolls have been re-dressed. 20" Thumbelina, re-dressed: **$100.00 – 175.00.** 14" Tiny Thumbelina, re-dressed: **$95.00 – 125.00.**

Thumbelina: The photo shows a 20" Thumbelina doll with her original box. The doll has a plastic wind-up knob on her back. She is a crying version of Thumbelina with holes in her ears and on the back of her head. Her box indicates that she cries when she moves. The dress the doll is wearing is not original. 20" doll with box, re-dressed: **$275.00 – 350.00.**

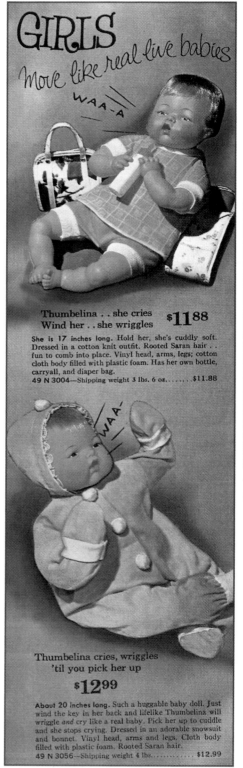

GIRLS *move like real live babies*

WAA-A

Thumbelina . . she cries Wind her . . she wriggles $11⁸⁸

She is 17 inches long. Hold her, she's cuddly soft. Dressed in a cotton knit outfit. Rooted Saran hair . . fun to comb into place. Vinyl head, arms, legs; cotton cloth body filled with plastic foam. Has her own bottle, carryall, and diaper bag.
49 N 3004—Shipping weight 3 lbs. 6 oz. $11.88

WAA-

Thumbelina cries, wriggles 'til you pick her up $12⁹⁹

About 20 inches long. Such a huggable baby doll. Just wind the key in her back and lifelike Thumbelina will wriggle *and* cry like a real baby. Pick her up to cuddle and she stops crying. Dressed in an adorable snowsuit and bonnet. Vinyl head, arms and legs. Cloth body filled with plastic foam. Rooted Saran hair.
49 N 3056—Shipping weight 4 lbs. $12.99

Tiny Thumbelina: Sears 1963 Christmas catalog showing two different sizes of Tiny Thumbelina.

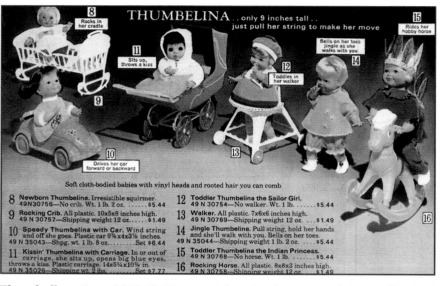

THUMBELINA . . only 9 inches tall . . just pull her string to make her move

8 Rocks in her cradle
11 Sits up, throws a kiss
15 Rides her hobby horse
14 Bells on her toes jingle as she walks with you
12 Toddles in her walker
9
10 Drives her car forward or backward
13
16

Soft cloth-bodied babies with vinyl heads and rooted hair you can comb

8 Newborn Thumbelina. Irresistible squirmer.
49N30756—No crib. Wt. 1 lb. 2 oz. $5.44
9 Rocking Crib. All plastic. 10x5x8 inches high.
49 N 30757—Shipping weight 12 oz. $1.49
10 Speedy Thumbelina with Car. Wind string and off she goes. Plastic car 9⅞x4x3⅛ inches.
49 N 35043—Shpg. wt. 1 lb. 8 oz. . . . . Set $6.44
11 Kissin' Thumbelina with Carriage. In or out of carriage, she sits up, opens big blue eyes, throws a kiss. Plastic carriage. 14x5¼x10⅛ in.
49 N 35026—Shipping wt. 2 lbs. . . . . Set $7.77

12 Toddler Thumbelina the Sailor Girl.
49 N 30754—No walker. Wt. 1 lb. $5.44
13 Walker. All plastic. 7x6x6 inches high.
49 N 30769—Shipping weight 12 oz. . . . $1.49
14 Jingle Thumbelina. Pull string, hold her hands and she'll walk with you. Bells on her toes.
49 N 35044—Shipping weight 1 lb. 2 oz. $5.44
15 Toddler Thumbelina the Indian Princess.
49 N 30768—No horse. Wt. 1 lb. $5.44
16 Rocking Horse. All plastic. 8x8x3 inches high.
49 N 30758—Shipping weight 12 oz. $1.49

Thumbelina: Sears 1970 Christmas catalog showing some of the smaller-sized Newborn and Toddler Thumbelina dolls available.

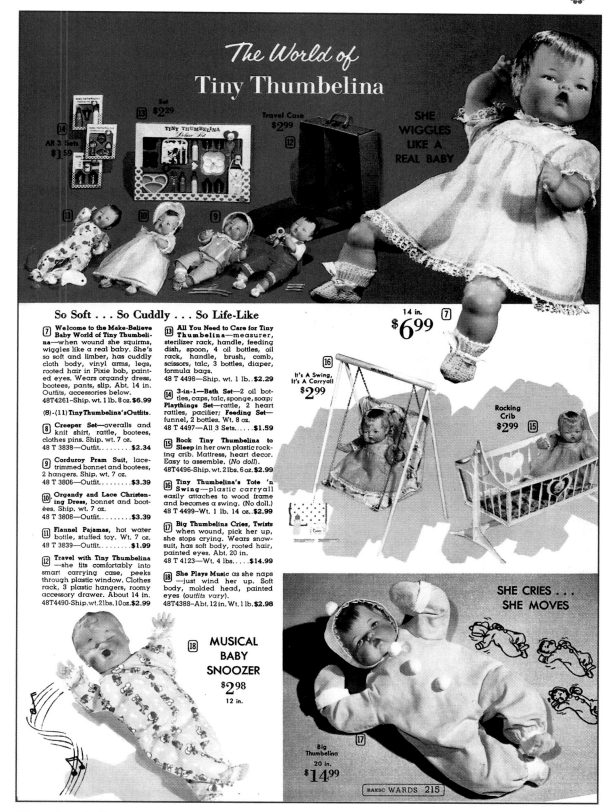

The World of

Tiny Thumbelina

All 3 Sets $1⁵⁹ ⑭

Set $2²⁹ ⑬

Travel Case $2⁹⁹ ⑫

SHE WIGGLES LIKE A REAL BABY

14 in. ⑦ $6⁹⁹

So Soft . . . So Cuddly . . . So Life-Like

⑦ **Welcome to the Make-Believe Baby World of Tiny Thumbelina**—when wound she squirms, wiggles like a real baby. She's so soft and limber, has cuddly cloth body, vinyl arms, legs, rooted hair in Pixie bob, painted eyes. Wears organdy dress, bootees, pants, slip. Abt. 14 in. Outfits, accessories below.
48T4261–Ship. wt. 1 lb. 8 oz. **$6.99**

(8)-(11) Tiny Thumbelina's Outfits.

⑧ **Creeper Set**—overalls and knit shirt, rattle, bootees, clothes pins. Ship. wt. 7 oz.
48 T 3838—Outfit **$2.34**

⑨ **Corduroy Pram Suit**, lace-trimmed bonnet and bootees, 2 hangers. Ship. wt. 7 oz.
48 T 3806—Outfit **$3.39**

⑩ **Organdy and Lace Christening Dress**, bonnet and bootées. Ship. wt. 7 oz.
48 T 3808—Outfit **$3.39**

⑪ **Flannel Pajamas**, hot water bottle, stuffed toy. Wt. 7 oz.
48 T 3839—Outfit **$1.99**

⑫ **Travel with Tiny Thumbelina**—she fits comfortably into smart carrying case, peeks through plastic window. Clothes rack, 3 plastic hangers, roomy accessory drawer. About 14 in.
48T4490–Ship. wt. 2 lbs. 10 oz. **$2.99**

⑬ **All You Need to Care for Tiny Thumbelina**—measurer, sterilizer rack, handle, feeding dish, spoon, 4 oil bottles, oil rack, handle, brush, comb, scissors, talc, 3 bottles, diaper, formula bags.
48 T 4498—Ship. wt. 1 lb. **$2.29**

⑭ **3-in-1—Bath Set**—2 oil bottles, caps, talc, sponge, soap; **Playthings Set**—rattle, 2 heart rattles, pacifier; **Feeding Set**—funnel, 2 bottles. Wt. 8 oz.
48 T 4497—All 3 Sets **$1.59**

⑮ **Rock Tiny Thumbelina to Sleep** in her own plastic rocking crib. Mattress, heart decor. Easy to assemble. (*No doll*).
48T4496–Ship. wt. 2 lbs. 6 oz. **$2.99**

⑯ **Tiny Thumbelina's Tote 'n Swing**—plastic carryall easily attaches to wood frame and becomes a swing. (No doll.)
48 T 4499—Wt. 1 lb. 14 oz. **$2.99**

⑰ **Big Thumbelina Cries, Twists** when wound, pick her up, she stops crying. Wears snowsuit, has soft body, rooted hair, painted eyes. Abt. 20 in.
48 T 4123—Wt. 4 lbs. **$14.99**

⑱ **She Plays Music** as she naps —just wind her up. Soft body, molded head, painted eyes (*outfits vary*).
48T4388–Abt. 12 in. Wt. 1 lb. **$2.98**

⑯ **It's A Swing, It's A Carryall** $2⁹⁹

⑮ **Rocking Crib** $2⁹⁹

⑱ MUSICAL BABY SNOOZER $2⁹⁸ 12 in.

SHE CRIES . . . SHE MOVES

⑰ **Big Thumbelina** 20 in. $14⁹⁹

BAXSC WARDS 215

Tiny Thumbelina: Montgomery Wards 1963 Christmas catalog showing some of the clothing and accessories available for Tiny Thumbelina.

In a Minute! Thumbelina: 9" pull-string doll that moves her arms up and down like a bouncing baby. She originally came with a high chair, a cup, spoon, and dish. When one of her small accessories is placed in her hand it bangs "impatiently" on the tray of her high chair. In a Minute! Thumbelina was available around 1971. The doll is marked "1970 Ideal Toy Corp./TT-9-H-175/Hong Kong" on her head and tagged "IN A MINUTE Thumbelina Ideal/all new material/Polyurethane Foam/Made in Hong Kong" on her body. MIB: **$95.00 – 125.00.** *Courtesy Nancy Ruppenthal.*

In a Minute! Thumbelina: The Thumbelina doll in the photo is wearing her original outfit but is missing her bib. Loose doll in original jumpsuit, no accessories: **$25.00 – 30.00.**

Tammy: Beginning in 1962 Ideal issued a teenage fashion doll called Tammy. Following Tammy's success, Ideal issued a family for her including a mother, a father, a brother, and a little sister. Several other friends in the line followed them. Numerous versions and variations of the dolls were issued, so only a few examples are shown here. This photo shows a straight-legged Tammy wearing her Nurse's Aide outfit which was sold separately for her. She is marked "©IDEAL TOY CORP. BS-12" on her head and "©IDEAL TOY CORP. BS-12/3" on her back (last digit varies on Tammy dolls). MIB: **$55.00 – 75.00.** Loose doll: **$25.00 – 40.00.** Outfit only/almost complete: **$50.00 – 75.00.**

Tammy: This photo shows a straight-legged Tammy wearing an unnamed blouse and pedal pushers sold separately as "switchables." This Tammy is marked "©IDEAL TOY CORP. BS-12" on her head and "©IDEAL TOY CORP. BS-12/1" on her back. MIB: **$55.00 – 75.00.** Loose doll: **$25.00 – 40.00.** Outfit only: **$30.00 – 45.00.**

Tammy: A Tammy doll with a top braid wearing an unnamed blouse and pedal pushers sold as "switchables." Most Tammy dolls with the top braid are Pos'n Tammy dolls with poseable legs, but this doll is an unusual straight-leg variation and could have been a transitional doll. She is marked "©IDEAL TOY CORP. BS-12" on her head and "©IDEAL TOY CORP. BS-12/1" on her back. Doll: **$25.00 – 40.00.** Outfit: **$30.00 – 45.00.**

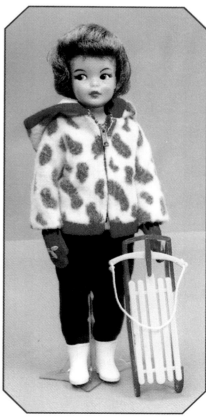

Pepper: Tammy's freckled-face little sister Pepper is 9¼" tall. Like Tammy, she came in several hair colors and styles. The doll shown in the photo is Pos'n Pepper wearing her Flower Girl outfit sold separately for her. Pepper is marked "©IDEAL TOY CORP. G9-E" on her head and "©IDEAL TOY CORP. G-9-W/1" (last digit varies on Pepper dolls) on her back. Loose doll: **$20.00 – 25.00.** Outfit alone, mint/complete: **$35.00 – 50.00.**

Pepper: This 1965 straight-leg Pepper has a trimmer body and smaller face than the earlier standard Pepper dolls. Here the new 1965 Pepper is shown with her Snow Flake outfit which was sold separately for her. Loose doll without outfit: **$25.00 – 30.00.** Mint and complete outfit including mittens and sled: **$45.00 – 75.00.**

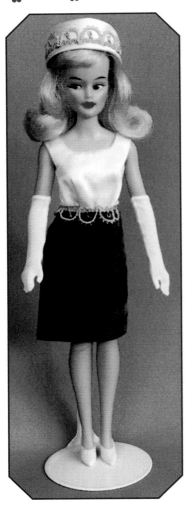

Misty: Tammy's best friend was Misty. The straight-leg, platinum blond version was called Glamour Misty, the Miss Clairol Doll. She featured hair which could be colored with special hair color applicators. Other Misty dolls sported light brown hair in a shoulder-length style or a long flip curl and came with either straight legs or a posing leg version called Pos'n Misty. 12" Misty is marked "©1965 Ideal Toy Corp. W-12-3" on her head and "©1965 Ideal (in circle) M-12" with a single digit number on her lower body. The straight leg Misty doll in the photo is wearing the dress and accessories to On The Town one of the outfits sold separately for her and Tammy. The outfit is not shown with the jacket that also came with it. Loose doll: **$25.00 – 45.00.** Outfit mint and complete: **$65.00 – 95.00.**

Misty: The straight-leg short-haired Misty doll in the photo is wearing Career Girl one of the outfits sold separately for her and Tammy. Loose doll: **$25.00 – 45.00.** Outfit mint and complete: **$65.00 – 80.00.**

Pos'n Misty: Pos'n Misty wearing Opening Night, one of the outfits sold separately for her and Tammy. Loose doll: **$25.00 – 45.00.** Outfit mint and complete: **$65.00 – 80.00.**

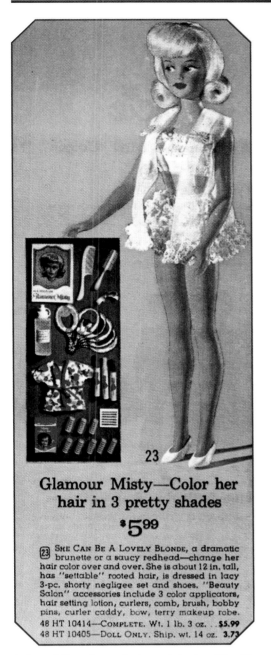

Glamour Misty—Color her hair in 3 pretty shades

$5⁹⁹

23 SHE CAN BE A LOVELY BLONDE, a dramatic brunette or a saucy redhead—change her hair color over and over. She is about 12 in. tall, has "settable" rooted hair, is dressed in lacy 3-pc. shorty negligee set and shoes. "Beauty Salon" accessories include 3 color applicators, hair setting lotion, curlers, comb, brush, bobby pins, curler caddy, bow, terry makeup robe.
48 HT 10414—COMPLETE. Wt. 1 lb. 3 oz. . .$5.99
48 HT 10405—DOLL ONLY. Ship. wt. 14 oz. 3.73

Misty: Misty shown in her original outfit with some of her hair accessories. The doll could be purchased with or without the accessories.
Montgomery Wards 1966 Christmas Catalog.

Dodi: Pepper's friend Dodi had below-the-shoulders ash blond or auburn hair parted to one side and clipped with a barrette. She had blue side-glance eyes with two painted corner lashes, and an open smile with painted teeth. She came with straight plastic legs or poseable vinyl legs. The straight-leg Dodi in the photo is marked "©1965 Ideal Toy Corp. D0 9-E" on her head and "©1964 Ideal Toy Corp. D0-9" on her back with a single digit underneath. Loose doll: **$15.00 – 20.00.**

Pos'n Dodi: Pos'n Dodi with bendable vinyl legs came dressed in a hip-long sleeveless pink knit shirt with a pink and white gingham ruffle, pink and white gingham slacks, and white shoes. Like the standard straight-leg Dodi, she came with either ash blond or auburn hair. Pos'n Dodi is marked "©1964 Ideal Toy Corp. D0 9-E" on her head and "©1964 Ideal Toy Corp. D0-9" on hip with a single digit on her buttocks. NRFB: **$50.00 – 65.00.** *Courtesy Sally Seikel.*

Betsy Wetsy/Betsy Baby: The name Betsy Wetsy was used by Ideal from 1937 through the 1980s, and was even reissued in recent years. Over the years the doll called Betsy Wetsy went through so many transformations. She often didn't look like the same doll from one version to the next. Some of the dolls were called Betsy Wetsy while others were given variations of Betsy's name like Betsy Baby, Little Betsy Wetsy, Big Baby Betsy Wetsy, Tiny Betsy Wetsy, and Tearie Betsy Wetsy. Betsy Wetsy dolls ranged in sizes from 8" to 25". To complicate matters Ideal made a Teary Deary doll using the same mold as their 1965 Betsy Wetsy. Shown in the photo are four different Betsy Wetsy or Betsy Baby dolls. From left to right:

13" platinum blond doll marked "©1965/IDEAL TOY CORP./TD14-W PAT. PEND." on her head and "©IDEAL TOY CORP/T-D-14" on her back. 17" platinum blond doll marked "©1965/IDEAL TOY CORP./TD-16-W-2 PAT. PEND" on her head and "©IDEAL TOY CORP/T-D-18" on her back. 15" dirty blond doll marked "©IDEAL TOY CORP./BW-16-L" on her head, and "©IDEAL TOY CORP/BW-15" on her back. 12" dirty blond doll marked "©1965/IDEAL TOY CORP/0-BW 13-L" on her head and "©IDEAL TOY CORP/BW 13" on her back. All the dolls in the photo have been re-dressed. Re-dressed: **$25.00 – 35.00.**

Betsy Wetsy/Betsy Baby: Close-up of the 15" doll shown in the previous photo. She is marked "©IDEAL TOY CORP./BW-16-L" on her head, and "©IDEAL TOY CORP/BW-15" on her back. **$25.00 – 35.00.**

Betsy Wetsy: A 13" molded-hair Betsy Wetsy doll. The molded-hair dolls seem to be just a little harder to find then the rooted hair dolls, although they aren't considered rare. Her head and limbs are vinyl and her torso is a soft plastic. She is marked "©IDEAL TOY CORP./BW-13" on both her head and back. The doll in the photo has been re-dressed. Re-dressed: **$30.00 – 45.00.**

Little Lost Baby: 22" doll with three different faces. The doll's head turns with a dial in the back of the head. **$35.00 – 55.00.** *Courtesy Robin Engle-hart, vintagelane.com, photo by Nancy Jean Mong.*

Pebbles and Bamm-Bamm: Ideal made a number of different sizes of Pebbles and Bamm-Bamm dolls. Depending on the size, Ideal called them by different names. The 8" dolls were called Baby Pebbles and Baby Bamm-Bamm. The 12" dolls were called Tiny Pebbles and Tiny Bamm-Bamm. The soft-bodied 14½" Pebbles was also called Baby Pebbles. The 16" dolls were simply called Pebbles and Bamm-Bamm. The photo shows different sizes of each doll. The smallest dolls are 8", the middle sized dolls are 12". The soft-bodied Pebbles in the back is 14½" and the large Bamm-Bamm in the back is 16". There was also a 16" plastic body Pebbles doll made. All the Bamm-Bamm dolls in the photo are missing their original hats, clubs, and bones in the front of their outfits, and the Pebbles dolls all originally came with a bone in their hair. Values listed on the lower end are for loose dolls without their complete original outfits, while dolls completely original with all accessories are on the higher end of the listed values. 8" dolls: **$20.00 – 40.00 each.** 12" dolls: **$25.00 – 50.00 each.** 14½" doll: **$65.00 – 85.00 each.** 16" dolls: **$50.00 – 85.00 each.**

Bamm-Bamm: 8" Baby Bamm-Bamm in his Flintstone Cave House. Rare when found still in his cave. MIB: **$200.00 – 225.00.** *Courtesy Michele Casino.*

Bamm-Bamm: 12" Tiny Bamm-Bamm with his original box. Tiny Bamm-Bamm is marked "©HANNA BARBERA PRODS.,INC./IDEAL TOY CORP./BB-12" on his head and back. MIB: **$150.00 – 175.00.** *Courtesy Michele Casino.*

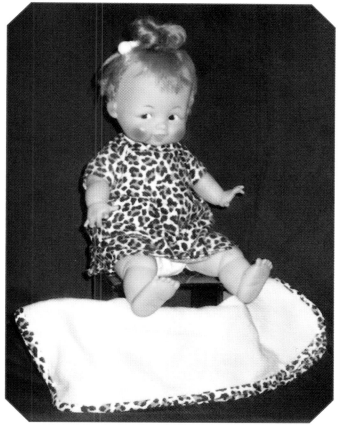

Pebbles: 14½" Baby Pebbles doll and her original box. This version of Pebbles has a stuffed cloth body and vinyl head and limbs. She came with a yellow flannel blanket with leopard print trim that matched her original outfit. The doll is marked "©HANNA BARBERA PRODS.INC/IDEAL TOY CORP./FS-14" on her head. MIB: **$150.00 – 280.00.** *Courtesy Michele Casino.*

Pebbles and Bamm-Bamm: 16" Pebbles and 16" Bamm-Bamm dolls with their original outfits. Pebbles, all original: **$50.00 – 85.00.** Bamm-Bamm, near mint, all original with hang tag: **$65.00 – 95.00.** *Courtesy Dawn Thomas.*

Pebbles and Bamm-Bamm: 12" Pebbles and 12" Bamm-Bamm dolls. Pebbles is missing her original bone in her hair and Bamm-Bamm is missing his original hat, club, and bone in his suit. 12" Pebbles or Bamm-Bamm, played with condition: **$35.00 – 45.00 each.**

Hong Kong doll: The 11" doll in the center of the photo is a cross between a Bamm-Bamm doll and a Pebbles doll. The doll appears to have been made using the Bamm-Bamm face mold and the Pebbles arms and leg molds. The doll's head is made of a light vinyl and the body and limbs are made of a thin plastic. The doll is marked with a symbol on his back that looks like "T.T." written in the middle of two semi-circles with a line coming out of the top of the inner semi-circle and going through the outer one. Below that is marked "MADE IN HONG KONG." The markings on the doll's head have been scratched out but the few partial letters or digits that can still be made out match those markings appearing on the 12" Bamm-Bamm doll standing next to him. Scratching out the original markings on a mold appears to be common practice when doll molds from one company are later used by another. The outfit the doll is wearing is Bamm-Bamm's and not original to him. Re-dressed Hong Kong Bamm-Bamm-like doll: **$15.00 – 20.00.**

Dino Doll Ride-On Toy: This is a rare ride-on toy sold separately for Pebbles and Bamm-Bamm dolls. The doll shown on Dino is a 12" Pebbles. Loose, no box: **$100.00 – 150.00.** *Courtesy Michele Casino.*

Pebbles Flintstone Cradle: This cradle was sold separately for Ideal's Pebbles doll. A doll was not included with the cradle. The cradle was meant to use with the 8", 12", or 14½" Pebbles dolls, but realistically only the 8" doll was small enough to actually lie down in it. MIB: **$100.00 – 150.00.** *Courtesy Michele Casino.*

[E] or [F]
4.99
Each

[E]   [F]

Winsome Twin Dolls

Winsome Twin Dolls: These two 14" Toddler Boy and Toddler Girl dolls were sold as Bob and his unnamed twin sister in the J.C. Penney 1971 Christmas catalog. Although the actual manufacturer is unknown, the dolls look as if they were made using the Ideal Pebbles head and body molds. No examples of these Pebble-like dolls have been spotted to accurately determine a value for them. *J.C. Penney 1971 Christmas catalog.*

Lolli-Pop Girl: A 1963 Sears catalog shows an 18" doll called Lolli-Pop Girl who appears to have been made using the Pebble's head mold. Like the doll at left, no examples of these Pebble-like dolls have been found. *Sears 1963 Christmas Catalog.*

Lolli-Pop Girl

7 Exclusive with Sears . . lovely lass waits gleefully to share her lolli-pop with some little girl. All vinyl. Fully jointed, molded plastic body with moving arms, legs and head. Rooted Saran hair. Dressed in flared top, long pants, matching slipper-socks. 18 inches tall.

Shipping weight 2 pounds.

49 N 3416..$9.66

7
$9.66

Tubsy: 16½" Tubsy was a battery-operated doll who would splash with her hands and turn her head when placed in a tub of water. She came with her own plastic tub for bathing. Her tub had a removable plastic cover so that the covered bathtub could be used as a dressing table. Although Tubsy was available for several years, the doll in the photo was sold in 1968 and was called Playtime Tubsy. She came with a pink kimono and diaper and the plastic toy shown in the front of the tub. Most Tubsy dolls came wearing a terry towel bunting in a variety of colors and did not have the plastic toy. The plastic toy had magnets inside and Tubsy would reach towards it. The doll is marked "©1966/IDEAL TOY CORP./BT-E-16-H79" on her head and "©1967/IDEAL TOY CORP./BT-18/2" on her back. On the back of the battery cover reads "WATER LINE" with a line above it, indicating that the doll shouldn't be placed in water any deeper than the line shown. Doll with tub and original outfit and toy: **$95.00 – 125.00.**

Tubsy: Close-up of Tubsy showing her adorable smile.

Tubsy: Two different versions of Tubsy. The doll on the left has lighter blond hair and painted teeth and the doll on the right has darker blond hair and molded teeth. Both dolls have the same markings. Doll on the left has been re-dressed. Loose dolls, no tub: **$35.00 – 50.00** (higher end if working condition).

Tubsy: The two Tubsy dolls on the left have lighter blond hair and painted teeth, while the two dolls on the right have darker blond hair and molded teeth. All but the doll on the right have all been re-dressed. Loose dolls, no tub: **$35.00 – 50.00** (higher end if working condition).

Tubsy Outfit: Tubsy had six outfits sold separately. Here she is wearing her Creeper Outfit. The original package shows the outfit having four felt appliqué people on the front but the actual outfit had three felt giraffes. MIB outfit: **$20.00 – 30.00.**

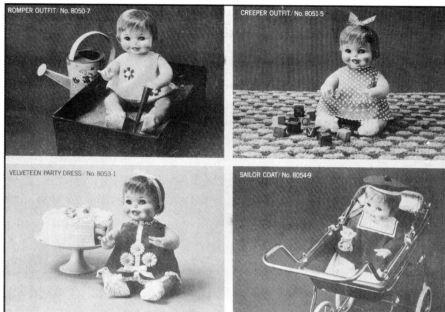

SLEEPER OUTFIT / No. 8052-3

ROMPER OUTFIT / No. 8050-7

CREEPER OUTFIT / No. 8051-5

VELVETEEN PARTY DRESS / No. 8053-1

SAILOR COAT / No. 8054-9

ORGANDY PARTY DRESS AND SLIP / No. 8055-6

Tubsy Outfit: The back of the package from Tubsy's Creeper Outfit shows all six outfits available for Tubsy. They included Romper Outfit, No. 8050-7; Creeper Outfit, No. 8051-5; Sleeper Outfit, No. 8052-3, Velveteen Party Dress, No. 8053-1; Sailor Coat, No. 8054-9; and Organdy Party Dress and Slip, No. 8055-6.

Real Live Lucy: This doll has a weight on the bottom of her neck causing her head to bob around. She also has a magnet inside her mouth. When her special magnetic spoon with molded spinach on it is offered to her she turns her face away from it but when she is offered her bottle, she turns eagerly towards it. In 1966 Sears Christmas catalog spelled the doll's name Lucy while Montgomery Wards spelled it Luci. The proper spelling of her name according to her original box is with a "y." Lucy has two molded teeth protruding from her mouth. The 20" doll is marked "©1965 /IDEAL TOY CORP./FL20-E-H33" on her neck. She is shown in her original dress but is missing her original booties. **$75.00 – 95.00.**

Real Live Lucy: Two Real Live Lucy dolls wearing variation dresses. The doll on the left has a felt appliqué puppy on the front while the doll on the right has the puppy printed on the material. Real Live Lucy's dress was also issued in blue with a pink felt puppy on her apron. **$75.00 – 95.00.**

Little Lucy, the Real Life Doll: This doll is a smaller version of Real Live Lucy. Like the larger size Lucy, this doll has a weight on the bottom of her neck causing her head to swivel. She is 13½" with open and shut eyes, three painted eyelashes in the corners, and molded eyelashes above her eyelids (missing from doll in photo). She is wearing her original outfit but is missing her original hat and booties. Some dolls have been found wearing a solid pink outfit with a felt giraffe on the front. Marks: "©1967/IDEAL TOY CORP./FL-13-H90" on head and "©1966/IDEAL TOY CORP./RB 13" on buttocks. She is harder to find than the larger size Real Live Lucy doll but her value is lower since there is less interest. **$55.00 – 75.00.**

Baby Lu: Like the previous two dolls, this doll has a weight on the bottom of her neck causing her head to swivel around. Baby Lu came with a spoon with spinach on it, which she would turn her face away from if offered it, and a bottle of milk which she would turn her face towards. This 13½" doll has two molded teeth and painted eyes that look very much like Ideal's Pebbles or Tabitha dolls. Other than the painted eyes, she is pretty much the same doll as the Little Lucy. She is marked "©1966/IDEAL TOY CORP./RB13-1-H56" on her head and has the same markings on her buttocks as the Little Lucy doll "©1966/IDEAL TOY CORP./RB 13." The doll in the photo has been re-dressed. Loose re-dressed doll: **$45.00 – 50.00.**

BABY LU
in her Shoofly Rocker

Offer her a spoon of spinach, she turns her head away .. but turns to milk like a good baby

$9⁹⁴

Like a living doll .. she turns her head from side to side, and bobs it up and down. Refuses "spinach," but loves her bottle! Rock her gently in cute plastic Shoofly. Soft vinyl 13-inch doll .. painted eyes. Rooted hair you can wash and comb. Lace-trimmed sun outfit, bonnet.
49 N 3070—Wt. 2 lbs. 12 oz..... $9.94

When you spank me here→ .. I cry WA-A-A

BABY SPANK ME
She sheds real tears

$6²²

When you spank, she fusses like a real baby. Feeds from her own bottle, too .. and what an appetite she has. Soft rooted hair .. sleeping eyes .. soft chubby arms. Vinyl. Dressed in bright red play outfit. 20 inches tall.
Shipping wt. 2 lbs. 4 oz.
49 N 3126........$6.22

Only Sears has **BABY BOO** with Bedroom Set

She stops crying when you cover her or turn off light

$14⁹⁹ without batteries

Pacifier stops her crying too .. no buttons to press. Soft polyethylene .. 21 in. tall, rooted hair, eyes close. 23-inch bed, handy night table. Romper, booties, bow. Order 2 "D" batteries, page 519.
79 N 3029C—Shpg. wt. 6 lbs...... Set $14.99

REAL LIVE LUCY
Nods her head and turns it from side to side

$13⁷⁹

Lively doll bobs her head around when you pick her up. Turns away from her spoon, but takes to her bottle right away! 20 in. tall. Jointed vinyl, rooted hair.
79 N 3051C—Wt. 4 lbs. $13.79

BABY PATTABURP
by Mattel

Pat her back gently to hear her burp

$7⁹⁹

Feed her, place her on your shoulder, pat her back .. she burps. Rooted hair. Soft body. Eyes close. Dressed in pink dress, panties, bootees. 16 in. tall. Feed her .. milk disappears .. then bottle refills.
Shipping weight 2 lbs. 4 oz.
49 N 3119.......... $7.99

Her Playall changes into 6 different dolly playthings

$11²²

SNUGGLEBUN and her PLAYALL 6
Baby Snugglebun .. a darling doll. Pick her up, she says "Mama." You can comb rooted hair .. eyes open and close. 15 in. tall of plastic and jointed to be movable. Striped dress. Her Playall 6 is wonderful! It can be a swing, playpen, stroller, high chair, rocker or car seat.
79 N 3059C—Shipping weight 5 pounds............. $11.22

$4⁹⁹

I'm COLORFUL CINDY .. color my bib and apron, wash them, color again. I drink and wet, too

Accent her red dress with whatever color suits your mood .. color the stenciled flower outline on her apron, or the kitten on her bib. 8 non-toxic, wash-off crayons. 16-inch fully-jointed vinyl baby doll has moving eyes, rooted hair. Baby bottle.
49 N 3078—Wt. 1 lb. 8 oz. $4.99

610 Sears BKMG

Baby Lu and her Shoofly Rocker: This Sears catalog page shows a painted-eye Baby Lu with her Shoofly Rocker and Real Live Lucy. *Sears 1966 Christmas Catalog.*

Real Live Lucy/Little Lucy/Baby Lu: Three different Ideal swivel head dolls. Each of these dolls has a weighted neck allowing their heads to bob around freely.

Goody Two Shoes: 19" battery-operated walking doll. The doll originally came with two pairs of shoes. Goody Two Shoes is marked "©1965/IDEAL TOY CORP./TW18-4-LH4" on her head and "©1965/IDEAL TOY CORP./WT 18/PAT.PENDING." on her back. Doll wearing original outfit: **$65.00 – 85.00.**

Talkin' Goody Two Shoes: This 27" doll sports a different look from Ideal's original 19" Goody Two Shoes doll. Talkin' Goody Two Shoes is taller and now has a toothy smile. This doll not only walks but she talks too. MIB and working: **$200.00 – 250.00.** *Courtesy Robin Englehart, vintagelane.com, photo by Nancy Jean Mong.*

90

Honeyball: Honeyball came with different hair colors and styles. Some Honeyball dolls are all vinyl as are the two dolls in the photo, while other Honeyball dolls have foam torsos and limbs that are poseable. The 9½" Honeyball is marked "©1966/IDEAL TOY CORP./M-9-H-74" on her head. The doll on the left is wearing her original dress. The doll on the right is wearing Ideal's Cinnamon's original dress. Loose doll with original dress: **$20.00 – 25.00.** *Courtesy Ann Wagner.*

Honeyball: Sears 1967 Christmas catalog shows Honeyball with a posing foam body as well as some of the outfits available for her. Her playroom case is advertised as a Sears exclusive.

HONEYBALL

She bends most any way .. even has a puppy $**3**⁹⁹

5 Fun's in store with Honeyball around. She can hang on a jungle gym, sit Indian fashion at a picnic. 9-in. body of soft vinyl foam makes her so limber. Rooted hair. In polka dot dress, she brings her soft vinyl puppy.
49 N 3202—Shpg. wt. 14 oz...$3.99

Honeyball Playroom Case $**4**⁷⁹
.. available only at Sears

6 Complete with bathtub and playpen. 2 drawers keep Honeyball's clothes handy. Colorful vinyl, about 15x6x12 inches high closed.
49 N 9249—Wt. 3 lbs. 14 oz...$4.79

Honeyball Playtime Outfits
.. available only at Sears

7 **Coat and Hat.** Orange velveteen .. lace trim, white collar, brim, pants.
49 N 3205—Shipping wt. 2 oz. $1.99

8 **Party Dress.** Crisp dotted swiss .. lace trim, scalloped velveteen collar. Slip, velveteen pants. Pert daisy hat.
49 N 3203—Shipping wt. 2 oz. $1.49

9 **Creeper Set.** Garden green overalls with rick rack trim. Posey print blouse. Straw cartwheel with ribbon.
49 N 3206—Shipping wt. 2 oz. $1.99

10 **Cat Pajamas.** She'll love bedtime in 1-pc. flannel P.J. Orange yarn tail, velveteen ears on matching hat.
49 N 3204—Shipping wt. 2 oz. $1.49

Dolls not included with outfits

SDI Sears 601

Crissy: A lot of youngsters growing up in the early 1970s played with Ideal's Beautiful Crissy with "growing" hair. Crissy had shoulder length red hair with a section of hair that came from a hole in the top of her head that could go from shoulder length down to her knees. Her hair grew by pushing a button on her belly and pulling on the growing section of hair. Turning a knob on her back could make her hair shorter again. Crissy was available starting in 1969 and continued to be sold through 1974. She was available again as Magic Hair Crissy in 1977. Many different versions of Crissy were produced along with a whole host of growing hair friends to go with her. Overall, Crissy enjoyed a relatively long market life for a doll. Because of her popularity years ago, she is relatively easy to find today. In spite of being common, prices for Crissy and all the Ideal grow-hair family of dolls has been steadily rising in recent years especially for mint in box dolls. Loose doll, all original: **$35.00 – 45.00.**

Mia: Another member of the Crissy grow-hair family, Mia is 15" tall and is marked "©1970/IDEAL TOY CORP./NGH-15-H173/HONG KONG" on her head and "©1970/IDEAL TOY CORP./GH-15/2M 5169-01" on her buttocks. Like all the dolls in the Crissy line she has hair that grows. She is shown here with her original box. Mint with box: **$65.00 – 85.00.**

Brandi: A member of the Crissy grow-hair family, Brandi is 17½" tall. She has a heart-shaped tattoo under her right eye. She is marked "48/©1971/IDEAL TOY CORP./GHB-18-H-185/HONG KONG" on her head, "©1971/IDEAL TOY CORP/MG-18/US PAT 3 162 976/OTHER PAT PEND./HONG KONG P" on her upper back, and "©1971/IDEAL TOY CORP/MG-18/HONG KONG P" on her lower back. In the photo Brandi is wearing a dress that was sold under two different names, Turned On Mini and Party Outfit. Doll with outfit: **$50.00 – 55.00.**

THEIR HAIR GROWS

Press each girl's tummy, then pull her rooted hair to make it "grow"... a knob on her back winds it short again

Mod Fashions for Crissy and Tressy

17½-inch Tressy $8.87

17½-inch Crissy $8.87

Introducing Velvet, Crissy's younger cousin. She's 15 inches tall.. looks so sweet, perky and almost real. With big violet eyes, silky rooted hair that grows to her knees, smooth vinyl skin. Jointed. Wt. 1 lb. 4 oz.
49 N 35028....$8.87

Outfits for Velvet

1 Lace-trimmed pajamas, peignoir. Shoes. Wt. 4 oz.
49 N 32551....$2.97

2 Mini-coat, cloche hat with pompon. Shoes. Wt. 4 oz.
49 N 32549....$2.97

15-in. $8.87 Velvet

Crissy's back again. Looking as spectacular as ever with her deep dark eyes and flowing auburn hair that's such fun to style. Vinyl; jointed; 17½ inches tall.
49 N 35041—Shpg. wt. 1 lb. 6 oz..............$8.87

Isn't Tressy a beauty? She's a glorious brunette with hair you'll love to style, vinyl flesh-look skin and large go-to-sleep eyes. Jointed; 17½ in. tall. With her own hair-styling accessories. Headband not incl.
49 N 35029—Shpg. wt. 1 lb. 6 oz..............$8.87

Outfits for Crissy and Tressy

3 Satin mini-dress, matching fringed scarf. Shoes.
49 N 32555—Shipping weight 4 oz. $2.97

4 Lace-trimmed bell-bottom pants, robe. Sandals.
49 N 30752—Shipping weight 5 oz. $2.97

5 Bell-bottoms, shirt, poncho. Peace medal, sandals.
49 N 32554—Shipping weight 4 oz. $2.97

6 Sparkly gold-color mini-dress, stockings, shoes.
49 N 32552—Shipping weight 4 oz. $2.97

7 Hooded cape with fur-look trim, pompons. Shoes.
49 N 30751—Shipping weight 5 oz. $2.97

NOTE: Dolls not included with outfits 1 through 7

Hair Care Kit. Styling brush, rollers, clips, pins, net, ponytail bands, bows, other decorations. Shpg. wt. 3 oz.
49 N 35042 ....$1.99

2-Doll Trunk. Vinyl. Hanger bar, hangers. Molded handle, metal clasp. 12x6½x20½-in. Dolls, accessories not included. Shpg. wt. 3 lbs.
79 N 35031C $3.99

Crissy/Velvet/Tressy: Three dolls from the Ideal Crissy line along with some of the outfits sold for them. *Sears 1970 Christmas Catalog.*

Posin' Cricket: 15½" Posin' Cricket was sold in 1971 and 1972. Her posing ability was limited to a jointed waist that allowed her to turn from one side to another. She usually has brown eyes, although some dolls have uncommon blue eyes. Cricket is one of the harder-to-find dolls from the Crissy family, especially in her original box with her original hair ornament. MIB: **$275.00 – 300.00.**

ElectroWoman Crissy: This 19" black Magic Hair Crissy doll was recycled into a new doll when she was dressed in an ElectroMan outfit and sold that way. The original ElectroMan figure was one of Ideal's toys that failed, much as the Magic Hair Crissy doll was not successful. It seems Ideal or perhaps even some other company that bought left-over stock matched up two of Ideal's failed products to create this doll. It is unconfirmed when exactly this doll was available but it's possible this doll may have been sold in the early 1980s. The doll is marked "©1977/Ideal Toy Corp./M.H.C-19-H-281/Hong Kong" on head and "©1974/Ideal (in circle)/Hollis, NY 11423" on body. The ElectroMan outfit is tagged "Hong Kong." The doll came in both white and black versions. White version: **$25.00 – 35.00.** Black version: **$35.00 – 50.00.** *Courtesy Ann Wagner.*

Harmony: A 21" tall music-making doll. Harmony came with a battery-operated amplifier that plugged into her back. When a record was placed inside the amplifier, Harmony's arms and head moved. Harmony is marked "H-200/©1971 IDEAL" (Ideal is circled) on her head and "©1972 IDEAL TOY CORP." on her back. MIB: **$95.00 – 145.00.** *Courtesy Mark A. Salyers.*

Harmony: Close-up of Harmony showing her lovely facial details. Her eyes are stationary with rooted eyelashes.

Flatsys: Flatsy dolls came in four sizes; 2½", 4¼", 4¾", and 8½". The 4¾" size Flatsys are the most common ones. Originally each poseable 4¾" vinyl Flatsy doll and his or her accessories were mounted on an illustrated cardboard backing and the set was framed with a plastic picture frame. The frame was placed in a cardboard base with the Flatsy name on it and both frame and base were sealed with cellophane. Some of the same Flatsy dolls that appeared in picture frames later were issued mounted on the cardboard background without the frame and packaged inside a white cardboard box instead of shrink-wrapped with the cardboard base. Some of the dolls were also issued inside oval lockets without their accessories. Loose Flatsy dolls generally run **$5.00 to $15.00 each.** In picture frames with accessories, values vary from **$35.00 to 95.00** depending on rarity of the set. Shown in the photo is 4¾" Nancy Flatsy. She is missing the baby that originally came inside the buggy. Incomplete set still mounted on frame without cellophane: **$35.00 – 40.00.** *Courtesy Robin Englehart, vintagelane.com, photo by Nancy Jean Mong.*

Ali Fashion Flatsy wearing Knit Mini. MIB: **$45.00 – 65.00.** *Courtesy Robin Englehart, vintagelane.com, photo by Nancy Jean Mong.*

Fashion Flatsy: Fashion Flatsy dolls were the tallest of the Flatsys measuring 8½". Each of the four Fashion Flatsys came dressed in several different outfits. Initially they were packaged in plastic frames with a cardboard backing, but towards the end of the line the dolls came inside white boxes. The cardboard backing upon which dolls were mounted remained the same. The photo shows Ali in her original box wearing Knit Mini and Gwen in her original box wearing Orange Raincoat & Boots. MIB: **$45.00 – 65.00.** *Courtesy Robin Englehart, vintagelane.com, photo by Nancy Jean Mong.*

Gwen Fashion Flatsy wearing Orange Raincoat & Boots. MIB: **$45.00 – 65.00.** *Courtesy Robin Englehart, vintagelane.com, photo by Nancy Jean Mong.*

Summer Mini Flatsy Collection: The 2½" Flatsy dolls known as Mini Flatsys are the hardest to locate. Mint-in-box or mint-in-frame sets are especially hard to find and in demand by Flatsy collectors. One group of Mini Flatsy dolls was the four seasons sets of Spring, Summer, Fall, and Winter. The sets came with three different framed Flatsy dolls portraying different scenes from the four seasons. Shown in the photo is the Summer Set. The set originally was sealed with cellophane on top of a cardboard base and had a sticker on the cellophane proclaiming the season it represented. Dolls in the first and third frames are missing their original hats. The doll with the yellow hair originally came in the middle frame and the black doll in the center originally came in the third frame that the yellow hair doll is in. **$80.00 – 100.00.**

Mini Flatsy: Photo shows the Fall Mini Flatsy set. Doll in first frame is missing her original hat. **$80.00 – 100.00.** *Courtesy Robin Englehart, vintagelane.com, photo by Nancy Jean Mong.*

Mini Flatsy: Like the regular size Flatsy dolls and the Fashion Flatsy dolls, some of the mini Flatsy dolls that first appeared in plastic frames were later issued mounted on their cardboard backgrounds and packaged inside white cardboard boxes. This photo shows a hard-to-find boxed set that combines two different miniature Flatsy sets that originally were sold separately in plastic frames with plastic clocks on the top. The set includes Slumber Time and Flower Time. Miniature Flatsy dolls are marked "IDEAL/©1969/PAT.PEND./ HONG KONG" on their backs. MIB: **$125.00 – 150.00.** *Courtesy Robin Englehart, vintagelane.com, photo by Nancy Jean Mong.*

Linda the Bendable Doll: An obvious Flatsy-copy, it's possible either the Flatsy molds or old stock of Flatsy dolls could have been bought out from Ideal by the company that put out these dolls. Company and year made is unknown. MOC: **$20.00 – 35.00.** *Courtesy Robin Englehart, vintagelane.com, photo by Nancy Jean Mong.*

Spinderella Flatsy: This doll, unlike other Flatsy dolls, came in a clear plastic dome. A pull string started her base to spin so she could dance. Spinderella Flatsy dolls came in yellow, pink, blue, and green versions. In the photo is a yellow version. Doll with dome case: **$35.00 – 50.00.** *Courtesy Robin Englehart, vintagelane.com, photo by Nancy Jean Mong.*

Play 'n Jane: This 15" battery-operated doll has red hair, green eyes, and came with numerous toys. The doll swings her arm to play horseshoes, tic-tac-toe, and basketball. Play 'n Jane is marked "©1971/IDEAL TOY CORP./TIC-16P-H-131/HONG KONG" on her head and "©1971/IDEAL TOY CORP./TIC-16" on her body. MIB with toys: **$65.00 – 75.00.** Doll alone: **$20.00 – 25.00.** *Courtesy Robin Englehart, vintagelane.com, photo by Nancy Jean Mong.*

Scribbles: 8" stuffed doll with vinyl hands. The sleeves of the dress were made for a child to place her fingers in, and then the child's fingers became the arms of the doll. The left hand of the doll had a hole in it where a piece of chalk was inserted. When a child moved her fingers, Scribbles could write, draw, or scribble on her blackboard. The doll came with a piece of chalk that was replaceable and a blackboard. Circa 1972. NRFB: **$65.00 – 75.00.** Doll alone: **$20.00 – 25.00.**

Belly Button Baby: 9" doll with a push button on his stomach that makes his arms, legs, and head move. MIB: **$30.00 – 45.00.**

Belly Button Baby: Side of Belly Button Baby's box showing the three different faces Belly Button Babies came with.

Tiffany Taylor: Tiffany Taylor had a rotating scalp that changed her hair from brunette to blond. 18" Tiffany Taylor is marked "©1973 IDEAL/ CG-19-H-230/HONG KONG" on her head and "©1974 IDEAL/ HOLLIS N.Y. 11423/2M-5854-01/1" on her lower body. NRFB: **$100.00 – 125.00.**

Tiffany Taylor: Black version of Tiffany Taylor. NRFB: **$100.00 – 150.00.** *Courtesy Hillary and Cliff James, Toy With Me.*

Tiffany Taylor: Tiffany Taylor as a brunette. MIB: **$85.00 – 100.00.** *Courtesy Robin Englehart, vintagelane.com, photo by Nancy Jean Mong.*

Tuesday Taylor: Like the larger size Tiffany Taylor, 11½" Tuesday Taylor also had a scalp that rotated to change her hair color from brunette to blond. Tuesday Taylor came in a number of different versions. She is marked "©1975/IDEAL/H-248/HONG KONG" on her head and "©1975/Ideal/U.S. Pat No. 399903640/HOLLIS N.Y. 11423/HONG KONG P" on her lower body. NRFB: **$45.00 – 55.00.** *Courtesy Sharon Wendrow, Memory Lane.*

Suntan Tuesday Taylor: This version of Tuesday Taylor not only had the scalp that rotated to change her hair color from brunette to blond but she also had skin that tanned when exposed to light. NRFB: **$45.00 – 55.00.** *Courtesy Sharon Wendrow, Memory Lane.*

Suntan Eric: Suntan Tuesday Taylor's boyfriend Eric. When he was placed in the sun he tanned within minutes. When he was removed from the sun he returned to normal. Suntan Eric is 12" tall and marked "©1976/IDEAL (circled)/HOLLIS N.Y. 11423/HONG KONG P" on his back. MIB: **$45.00 – 50.00.** Loose: **$20.00 – 25.00.**

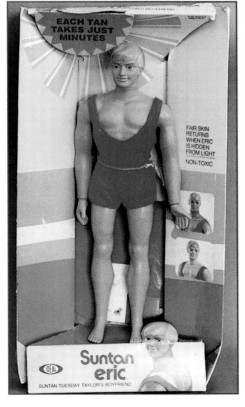

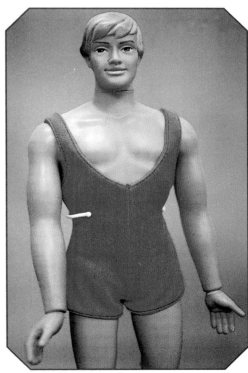

Jody, An Old Fashioned Girl: 9" doll with ankle-length hair. Jody could be purchased wearing one of several different outfits. The white version of Jody had red hair and the black version had black hair. Jody is marked "©1974/IDEAL/9G-H-/241" on her head and "©1974/IDEAL/HONG KONG" with a backwards digit underneath on her back. Shown in the photo is the black version of Jody wearing Party Formal. MIB: **$30.00 – 45.00.** *Courtesy Robin Englehart, vintagelane.com, photo by Nancy Jean Mong.*

Dorothy Hamill: A doll of Olympic skater Dorothy Hamill was made using the same body as Ideal's Tuesday Taylor. She came with a plastic skating rink that the doll could spin around on. Dorothy is marked "©1977 D.H./Ideal/H-282/HONG KONG" on her head and "©1975/Ideal/U.S. Pat No. 399903640/HOLLIS N.Y. 11423/HONG KONG P" on her lower body. NRFB: **$25.00 – 55.00.** *Courtesy Michele Casino.*

Andy Gibb: Singer Andy Gibb was made into a 7¼" doll by Ideal in 1979. Andy came with a white plastic stand so he could disco dance. The doll is marked "©1979/S.G.L. IDEAL/H-3177/HONG KONG" on his head and "ANDY GIBB™/IDEAL TOY CORP./HONG KONG" on his back. Little demand for this doll has so far kept his value down. MIB: **$20.00 – 40.00.** *Courtesy Robin Englehart, vintagelane.com, photo by Nancy Jean Mong.*

Imperial

Little Sweethearts: 3" Flatsy-type dolls from Imperial Toy Corp., 1973. MIP: **$10.00 – 12.00.** *Courtesy Robin Englehart, vintagelane.com, photo by Nancy Jean Mong.*

Italocremona

Jenni: 12½" Italian doll manufactured from the firm Italocremona around 1964. Her clothing was designed by fashion designer Emilio Schuberth who also designed a line of children's clothing. Her hair was styled by Alexandre of Paris. Mint with box: **$55.00 – 75.00.** *Courtesy Janet Lawrence and Mike Lawrence.*

Nina: Freckled face 11" doll has ice blue sleep eyes with long lashes. She is wearing her original pink corduroy dress with blue floral sleeves, and replaced shoes and socks. She is marked "©1965 Italocremona" on her head and "800/ MADE ITALY" on her back. **$20.00 – 30.00.** *Courtesy Robin Englehart, vintagelane.com, photos by Nancy Jean Mong.*

Miss America Pageant or Americas Pageant Doll: The Kaystan Pageant Doll Company of Mansfield, Massachusetts, put out a group of 14" Miss America Pageant dolls in the 1970s. An early advertisement for these dolls calls them Miss America Pageant dolls, however the sash found on the 1971 doll shown below reads "AMERICAS PAGEANT DOLL." It could be that the company may not have been authorized to use the Miss America name and may have changed the name of the dolls from Miss America Pageant to Americas Pageant. In any event, the author couldn't positively determine under what name the dolls were sold. The dolls came dressed in a pageant gown with a cape, a sash, a tiara on their head, gloves, and shoes. Underneath their pageant gowns they wore swimsuits.

1970 Americas Pageant Doll: This regal pageant doll strongly resembles Princess Grace of Monaco. Most likely the doll originally came with a sash similar to the one the doll in the photo on the right is wearing. Underneath her gown she is wearing a white swimsuit. The 14" doll has rooted eyelashes and is marked "KAYSTAN CO./19©70" on her head and "HONG KONG" on her body. **$25.00 – 35.00.**

1971 Americas Pageant Doll: Unlike the previous doll, this doll has painted eyelashes. Her sash reads "AMERICAS PAGEANT DOLL 1971." Underneath her gown she is wearing a white swimsuit. The 14" doll is marked "KAYSTAN CO./19©71" on her head and "HONG KONG" on her body. **$20.00 – 25.00.**

1972 Americas Pageant Doll: Most likely this doll originally came with a sash and crown similar to the ones the previous doll is wearing. She has single-stroke eyeliner in the outer corners of her eyes. Like the other two dolls, underneath her gown she is wearing a white swimsuit. She is also 14" and is marked "KAYSTAN CO./ 19©72" on her head and "HONG KONG" on her body. **$20.00 – 25.00.**

Americas Pageant Doll: Each Americas Pageant doll came wearing the same swimsuit under their gowns. Doll wearing swimsuit and shoes only: **$10.00 – 15.00 each.**

Americas Pageant Dolls: The Kaystan dolls look quite similar to Remco's Lisa Littlechap. Note the similarity of the Pageant doll's arms and hands to Lisa Littlechap's. Unfortunately, the Pageant dolls were not made with the same high quality vinyl as the Littlechap dolls.

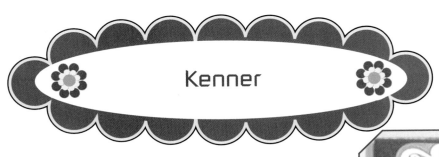

Kenner

Blythe: Kenner's Blythe is an unusual 11" fashion doll with an overly large plastic head on a petite vinyl body. Her eyes can be changed to four different colors with the pull string in her head. Blythe came with blond, brunette, red, or black hair, with bangs or with a side part. In addition, wigs in yellow, green, pink, and blue were also sold for her. Twelve different outfits were sold separately for her. Blythe dolls were originally sold wearing four of these different outfits. Brunette dolls were sold wearing either Medieval Mood or Golden Goddess, blonde dolls were sold wearing Pretty Paisley, and redheads were sold wearing Love 'N Lace. As with most dolls, it wouldn't be uncommon to find different combinations of hair color and outfits since most toy companies used up whatever supplies were available, especially towards the end of a line, and Kenner was probably no exception. Blythe dolls are marked "Blythe™/KENNER PRODUCTS/CINCINNATI, OHIO/©1972 GENERAL MILLS/FUN GROUP INC./PATENT PENDING/MADE IN HONG KONG" on their backs. In recent years Blythe has gained tremendous popularity with collectors and values for her have skyrocketed.

Blythe: Blond side-part Blythe wearing her Pretty Paisley dress. NRFB: **$3,000.00 – 4,000.00.** *Courtesy Lisa Petrucci.*

Blythe: Blythe with her original box shown wearing her Golden Goddess dress. Near mint with Box: **$1,200.00 – 1,500.00.** *Courtesy Robin Englehart, vintagelane.com, photo by Nancy Jean Mong.*

Blythe: Three different Blythe dolls wearing original Blythe outfits. From left to right: dark brunette Blythe with bangs wearing Medieval Mood, red haired side-part Blythe wearing Love 'n Lace, and medium brunette Blythe with bangs wearing Golden Goddess. **$500.00 – 700.00 each.** *Courtesy Lisa Petrucci.*

Blythe: A brunette Blythe with bangs showing her four different eye colors. **$500.00 – 700.00.** *Courtesy Jennie Brott.*

Blythe's Boutique: Blythe fashion Lounging Lovely in its original box. NRFB: **$125.00 – 175.00.** *Courtesy Robin Englehart, vintagelane.com, photo by Nancy Jean Mong.*

Blythe's Boutique: Blythe's Medieval Mood outfit in its original box. NRFB: **$125.00 – 175.00.** *Courtesy Robin Englehart, vintagelane.com, photo by Nancy Jean Mong.*

Blythe's Boutique: Blythe's Pinafore Purple in its original box. NRFB: **$125.00 – 175.00.**
Courtesy Robin Englehart, vintagelane.com, photo by Nancy Jean Mong.

Blythe Boutique: Back of one of Blythe's fashions shows some of the outfits and wigs available for her. *Courtesy Robin Englehart, vintagelane.com, photo by Nancy Jean Mong.*

Blythe's Fashion Wardrobe Case: Carrying case sold separately for Blythe. **$40.00 – 50.00.** *Courtesy Michele Casino.*

Garden Gal: Brunette Garden Gal Meadow. MIB: **$20.00 – 25.00.**

Garden Gal: 7" plastic doll from 1972 who "assisted" children in planting and growing flowers. Included with the doll was a seed packet, two flower pots, two peat discs, and a watering can. Children could have the doll hold the watering can and water the plants. There were three different Garden Gal dolls: a blond named Skye, a brunette named Meadow, and a red haired doll named Willow. The dolls are marked "GARDEN GAL/BY/KENNER/HONG KONG" on their backs. They had molded white painted boots. Shown in the photo is red haired Willow. MIB: **$20.00 – 25.00.**

Jenny Jones: Close-up of the mother doll, Jenny Jones. The outfit she is wearing was an additional one sold separately for her. *Courtesy Carole Lacy Bailey.*

Jenny Jones & Baby John: This 1973 mother and baby set came with two dolls, a baby crib with mattress, a baby bottle, instructions, and a white "x" stand for Jenny. 9" Jenny originally came dressed in a multicolored striped hostess gown, blue panties, and navy blue shoes. Jenny has bendable legs that click into several positions. 2½" Baby John came dressed in a pink top, yellow footed bottoms, and came with a blanket with the same stripes as those on his mother's dress. He drinks and wets and has rooted blond hair. Mint with box set: **$25.00 – 35.00.** *Courtesy Carole Lacy Bailey.*

Jenny Jones & Baby John: Baby John is shown with some of his and his mom's clothing. Jenny's outfit on the left was sold separately. The hostess dress on the right was the original dress Jenny came wearing. Baby John's clothing coordinated with his mom's outfits. *Courtesy Carole Lacy Bailey.*

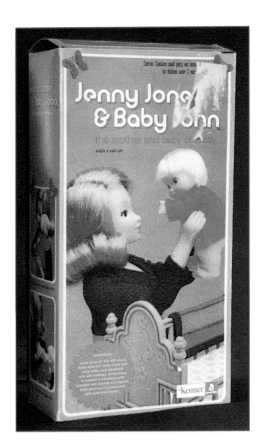

Jenny Jones & Baby John: Close-up the dolls' original box. *Courtesy Carole Lacy Bailey.*

Jenny Jones & Baby John: Back of the doll's original box showing some of the coordinating outfits which could be purchased separately for Jenny and baby John, as well as a nursery set that could also be purchased separately. *Courtesy Carole Lacy Bailey.*

Dusty: An action-oriented fashion doll, Dusty was touted as being a sports superstar. The 11½" doll has a jointed waist that when turned swivels quickly back allowing her to swing a bat, a tennis racket, or other sporting equipment. Shown here is a Dusty trade-in doll. This doll was available for $1.99 with the trade in of an old doll. Most examples of Dusty have bendable arms, jointed wrists, and hands that are cupped to grasp items, but this version doesn't have any of those features. Her hair is in a long shag, while most Dusty dolls come with a short shag hairstyle. Fashions for Dusty included outfits for tennis, golf, volleyball, softball, gymnastics, skiing, and many other sporting activities. Dusty was sold in either a swimsuit or a sporting outfit. She is marked "77/©G.M.F.G.I." on her head and "©1974 G.M.F.G.I. KENNER PROD./CINCINNATI, OHIO 45202/MADE IN HONG KONG" on her lower back. With original box **$30.00 – 40.00.**

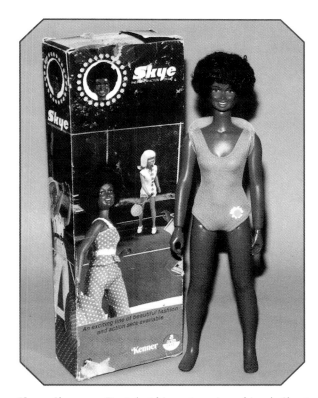

Skye: Skye was Dusty's African-American friend. She tends to be harder to find than Dusty. With original box: **$35.00 – 45.00.** *Courtesy Robin Englehart, vintagelane.com, photo by Nancy Jean Mong.*

DISGUISE FEMBOT* AS JAIME* OR... THE MYSTERY LADY.

Fembot: This character is Jamie Sommers's "deadliest" enemy from the show *The Bionic Woman*. The robot-like doll comes with two removable masks. The back of the box tells how without the masks the doll is Fembot, "evil and unfeeling with her mechanized mind." When the Jamie Sommers mask is placed on the doll's face, she becomes a Jamie Sommers double, or for an anonymous look a hairpiece is slipped over the doll's head to hide her real hair, and when the "mystery lady" mask is placed on the doll, Fembot becomes unrecognizable. This doll is hard to find. MIB: **$150.00 – 200.00.**

Baby Won't Let Go: This doll grasps tightly onto items. She is marked on her head "Hong Kong/C.M.F.G.I. 1977" and "C.M.F.G.I. 1977/KENNER PROD. DIV" along with an address on her back. MIB: **$25.00 – 35.00.** *Courtesy Robin Englehart, vintagelane.com, photo by Nancy Jean Mong.*

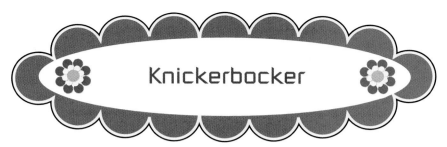

Holly Hobbie: In 1967 American Greetings introduced their new Holly Hobbie character on greeting cards. Named after the artist who created her, Holly Hobbie quickly captured the hearts of both children and adults. Before long American Greetings catapulted Holly Hobbie into the phenomenon of character licensing. The little girl with the oversized bonnet and patchwork pinafore began appearing on everything from tote bags to bedspreads. In the early 1970s Knickerbocker began manufacturing a large variety of Holly Hobbie dolls and toys. The Knickerbocker Holly Hobbie rag dolls shown here are 9" and 15½". The dolls themselves are not tagged, but their removable dresses are tagged, "The Original/HOLLY HOBBIE®/copyright©AMERICAN GREETINGS CORPORATION/ALL NEW MATERIALS/COTTON AND SYNTHETIC FIBERS" on one side (large doll also says "SURFACE WASHABLE ONLY" at end) and "KTC/KNICKERBOCKER/KNICKERBOCKER TOY COMPANY, INC./MIDDLESEX, NJ 08846 U.S.A./MADE IN TAIWAN, REPUBLIC OF CHINA." on the other side of the tag. **$15.00 – 25.00 each.**

Holly Hobbie: Three 10½" dolls. Their heads and limbs are vinyl and their torsos are plastic. From left to right in the photo are Holly Hobbie and her friends Carrie and Amy. The dolls are marked "K.T.C./© A.G.C./1974" on their heads and "HOLLY HOBBIE®/©AMERICAN GREATINGS/CORP.1974/MADE IN TAIWAN FOR/KNICKERBOCKER TOY/CO., INC." on their backs. These vinyl, plastic Holly Hobbie dolls tend to be harder to find than the cloth dolls. Loose dolls/played with condition: **$15.00 – 25.00 each.**

Amy: 6" Holly Hobbie friend Amy. She is all vinyl and marked "©K.T.C./A.G.C./MADE IN TAIWAN/1975" on her head and, "HOLLY HOBBIE®/©A.G.C. 1975/MADE IN TAIWAN/ K.T.C." on her back. She is wearing her original dress but is missing her original bonnet, apron, bloomers, stockings, and shoes. This doll originally came in a playset with a baby doll, carriage, and other small accessories. **$5.00 – 10.00.** *Courtesy Dal Lowenbein.*

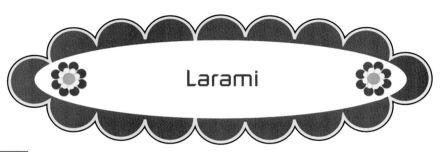

Larami

Bobby and Janie: When loose, Janie is often called a Barbie clone by collectors because of her similarity to the ponytail Barbie of the early 1960s. Bobby is similar to Barbie doll's boyfriend Ken right down to his red swimsuit with a white stripe down the side. Janie is 11" and has a molded plastic ponytail that easily pops out of the back of the head. Loose dolls often are missing the ponytail. Bobby is 11½". Exact markings of these dolls were not available at the time of publication, but they may be marked "Made in Hong Kong" on their backs. The front of their card reads "Parts marked with country of origin/packed and printed in U.S.A./No. 9035/Larami Corp., Phila., PA." Loose: **$5.00 – 10.00 each.** MOC set: **$20.00 – 30.00.**

Manufacturer Unknown

Little Debbi-Eve: The manufacturer of this 21" doll is unknown, but because of her similarities to the Melody Baby Debbi doll shown on page 248 of the first volume of *Dolls of the 1960s and 1970s,* it is a guess that she may have been made by the Skippy Doll Corporation. She is marked "S" on the back of her neck, however dolls from the Skippy Doll Corporation are usually marked "SD." Little Debbi-Eve has a vinyl head and plastic torso and limbs. Her wrist tag reads "LITTLE Debbi-Eve/A LITTLE MOTHER's DELIGHT." She has a ribbon pinned on the front of her outfit reading "HOLD MY LEFT HAND UP AND I WILL WALK WITH YOU." She came with a set of curlers. Her plain cardboard box gives no company information but does indicate that Little Debbie-Eve was issued with blond, brunette, platinum, or red hair and came wearing a blue or pink outfit. Year(s) the doll was available is unknown for sure but she probably dates from the early 1960s. Without her original clothing, hang tag, or box, this doll would be difficult to identify since her face is similar to many dolls from the same period. MIB with hang tags: **$50.00 – 65.00.** *Courtesy Gloria Telep.*

Charlotte: This handmade doll is a reproduction of author Laura Ingalls Wilder's childhood doll, which she wrote about in her *Little House on the Prairie* books. Over the years many different representations of the Charlotte doll have been offered through various sources. The doll in the photo was purchased through the Laura Ingalls Wilder fan club sometime around 1970 – 1971. No other examples of this version of Charlotte have been located to determine a fair market value. *Courtesy Karen Hickey.*

Little Girl's Jewelry: 1" doll inside a plastic pin or brooch very similar to Mattel's Jewelry Kiddles. A whole variety of different dolls came inside these pins. This is just one of them. They were made in Hong Kong. MOC: **$10.00 – 15.00.**

Little Girl's Jewelry: 1" doll inside a plastic ring similar to Mattel's Jewelry Kiddles. Like the pins, a whole variety of different dolls came inside the rings. MOC: **$10.00 – 15.00.**

Marx

Campus Cuties: Molded hard plastic figures that measure approximately 5½" to 6". The figures are dated in Roman numerals on the bottom MCMLXIV (1964) and include the name of the Campus Cutie. These figures came in pink but were reissued in a cream color later on, although the cream-colored figures are still dated 1964. Some painted sets of these figures have been spotted as well, but the author has not been able to verify when they came out. The eight Campus Cuties included Dinner for Two, Nitey Night, Lodge Party, Shopping Anyone?, On the Beach, On the Town, Lazy Afternoon, and Stormy Weather. Shown in the photo is Lodge Party. **$3.00 – 7.00.** *Courtesy Robin Englehart, photo by Cindy Sabulis.*

Campus Cuties: Campus Cutie Nitey Night. **$3.00 – 7.00.** *Courtesy Robin Englehart, vintagelane.com, photo by Nancy Jean Mong.*

114

Twinkie: Marx's Twinkie was billed as "The Teeny, Tiny Doll with the BIG Wardrobe." The molded plastic doll is 5" tall and is jointed at the hips, shoulders, and neck. She has painted socks and shoes. Her head is nearly bald with only a few molded strands of hair the same color as her skin. The idea was to use her wigs to change her hair color and style with each new outfit. Her clothing and accessories including her wigs were all made of a rubbery plastic. It is believed that all the sets included the same doll and the same clothing and accessories, but the clothing and accessories in different sets have been found in different color combinations. Some sets include brunette wigs, while others have black; some have blue clothing, others have pink, and so on. Items included in the Twinkie sets were:

1 doll	1 hat box (not in photo)
1 doll stand	1 suitcase (not in photo)
6 wigs	1 fur stole
2 wig stands	1 scarf
4 dresses	1 poodle (not in photo)
2 skirts	2 panties
1 pair of shorts	1 sleeveless sweater/vest
1 halter top	1 nightie
2 handbags	1 pair of slippers
1 clutch purse	1 foldup wardrobe (not in photo).
2 hats	

Twinkie is often found still in her original box since so many owners used the box to hold all her accessories. With box and accessories: **$45.00 – 75.00.**

Twinkie: The two photos show the same 5" molded plastic Twinkie doll wearing two different removable wigs and two different outfits. She is marked "LOUIS MARX & CO. INC./MCMLXV" on her back. Doll alone: **$10.00 – 15.00.**

Twinkie: Twinkie's original box.

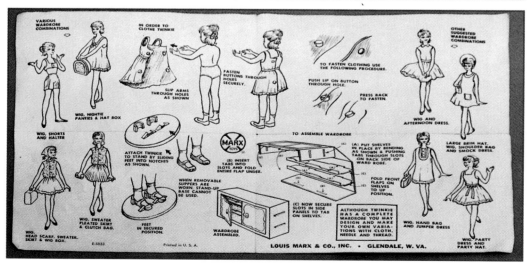

Twinkie: Twinkie's original instructions (front and back).

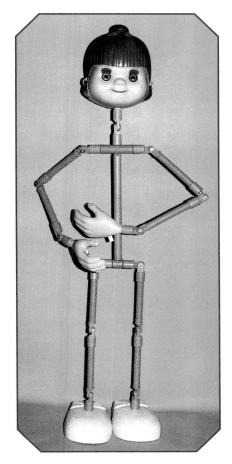

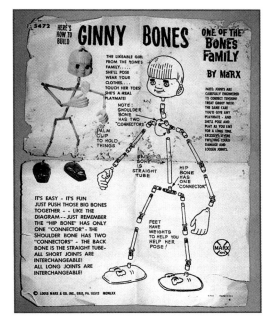

Ginny Bones: An unusual 3' tall doll that had to be put together. Ginny Bones had poseable pink "bones," and her feet were weighted so that she wouldn't topple over. On her box was printed "The foot bone connects to the ankle bone...the ankle bone connects to the leg bone...and so on...soon you have a real posin' pal!" Box and instructions are dated 1970 in Roman numerals. Other Bones family members included Ginny's brother, Skinny Bones, their dog Ham Bones, and an unnamed horse. Doll with original box: **$35.00 – 50.00.** *Courtesy Robin Englehart, vintagelane.com, photos by Nancy Jean Mong.*

Jane West: The dolls in the Best of the West line were considered action figures since they were primarily geared for boys who liked to play cowboys and Indians. The female members of the line helped entice girls to play with the figures as well. The Best of the West line was sold from 1973 to 1975. The figures are molded heavy vinyl with pin-jointed limbs and molded-on Western clothing as well as one to three removable articles of clothing made of a rubbery plastic. The figures came with approximately 20 – 35 small plastic accessories like guns, campfire cooking equipment, and horse equipment. Some figures could be purchased with or without horses and the horses were available separately as well. Johnny West was the most popular member of the line and the one most collectors are familiar with. Other members include his wife Jane West, his daughter Josie West, his son Jamie West, villain Sam Cobra, Fighting Eagle, Chief Geronimo, Chief

Cherokee, Princess Wildflower, Sheriff Garrett, Captain Maddox, scout Bill Buck, trooper Zeb Zachary, and General Custer. Values for any of the figures increase with the number of accessories included with them, and of course condition plays a large role in their value since many of them were heavily played with. In the photo is 11" Jane West. She is marked "MARX TOY/©/MCMLXXIII/MADE IN/U.S.A" in a circle on her back. The horse in the photo was sold separately, but another Jane West set did come with a horse. MIB: **$65.00 – 95.00.** *Courtesy Robin Englehart, vintagelane.com, photos by Nancy Jean Mong.*

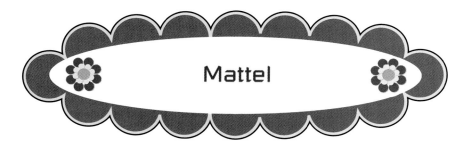

Mattel

Barbie: This #3 brunette doll is wearing a common but popular vintage Solo in the Spotlight outfit. Her pale white skin color is common in the first three issues of the Barbie doll. Vintage Barbie dolls often have the paint wearing off their lips, eyebrows, eyelids, and even eyes, and so many collectors choose to have their dolls' faces repainted completely or just touched up. When a Barbie doll has had any kind of restoration done to her facial paint, value would be lower than for a similar doll with her original face paint still in good shape. The doll in the photo has had her lips and eyebrows professionally redone. The #3 Barbie is marked "BARBIE™/PATS.PEND./©MCMLVIII/BY/MATTEL/INC." on her buttocks. Doll without outfit: **$500.00 – 800.00.** Outfit mint/complete: **$95.00 – 175.00.**

Barbie: In 1961 the ponytail Barbie doll was joined by a Barbie with a new bubble cut hairstyle. The earlier bubble cut Barbie dolls are marked "BARBIE®/PATS.PEND./©MC MLVIII/BY/MATTEL/INC." on their buttocks. Later bubble cut dolls are marked "MIDGE®/©1962/BAR-BIE®/©1958/BY/MATTEL, INC." Available in various shades, loose and nude bubble cut Barbie dolls can range in value anywhere from $35.00 to $250.00 depending on condition and uniqueness of the doll. Value also depends on what outfit they are wearing, if any. The doll in the photo has the MIDGE/BARBIE markings. She is wearing Bride's Dream. Loose doll: **$65.00 – 95.00.** Outfit, complete except necklace: **$65.00.**

Malibu Barbie: Most children who grew up in the 1970s remember Barbie looking like the doll in the photo. Mattel sold Malibu Barbie with the suntan skin from 1971 to 1976, so there is an abundance of these dolls floating around the collectors' market. Malibu Barbie has painted eyelashes, bendable knees, and a twist waist. She wore a one-piece blue swimsuit and came with a pair of sunglasses on her head and a yellow beach towel. Markings vary on the dolls. The earliest ones are marked "©1966/MATTEL, INC./U.S. PATENTED/U.S. PAT. PEND./MADE IN/JAPAN." Later Malibu Barbie doll's markings were similar but the last lines read made in Taiwan or Korea. Mint loose doll with original swimsuit and sunglasses: **$25.00 – 35.00.** *Courtesy Dal Lowenbein.*

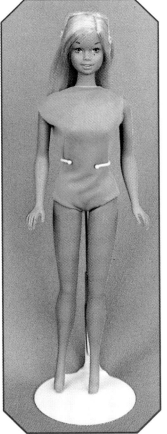

Barbie: After the straight-legs/molded lashes era of Barbie dolls, Barbie got an updated look in 1967 that included long straight hair, bendable legs, twist waist, and rooted eyelashes. This doll is called the Twist 'N Turn Barbie by collectors or referred to by the abbreviated name of TNT Barbie. The TNT Barbie dolls came in a large variety of hair colors. TNT Barbie dolls with red or titian hair like the doll in the photo are rare and are worth much more than dolls with more common hair colors. TNT Barbie dolls are marked "1966/MATTEL, INC./U.S. PATENTED/U.S. PAT.PEND./MADE IN/JAPAN" on their buttocks. Loose titian TNT doll with swimsuit and wrist tag: **$275.00 – 395.00.**

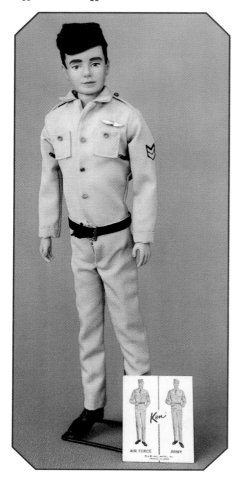

Ken: Barbie doll's 12" boyfriend Ken was introduced in 1961 and like Barbie continues to be made today. The first Ken dolls had flocked or fuzzy hair in either blond or brunette. Later Ken dolls were made with painted hair. A few issues of Ken were even made with rooted hair. The Ken doll shown here is the first version with flocked hair and straight legs. He is wearing his Army and Air Force outfit which was sold separately from 1963 to 1965. Flocked hair Ken is marked "KEN®/PATS.PEND./©MCMLX/BY/MATTEL./INC" on his buttocks. Ken doll without outfit: **$30.00 – 50.00.** Outfit mint/complete: **$45.00 – 65.00.**

Skipper: Barbie doll's little sister Skipper is 9" tall. She was issued with blond, red, or brunette hair. The earliest Skipper dolls had straight legs and are marked "SKIPPER/©1963/MATTEL, INC." on their buttocks. After Skipper's friends Skooter and Ricky starting using the same body as she did, the "SKIPPER" name was dropped from the markings so later Skipper dolls are marked "©1963/MATTEL, INC." on their buttocks. The straight-legged Skipper doll in the photo is wearing her Red Sensation outfit. Doll without fashion: **$35.00 – 55.00.** Outfit mint/complete: **$45.00 – 65.00.**

Barbie & Skipper: This red haired ponytail Barbie is shown wearing her Fancy Free dress from 1963 to 1964. Her little sister Skipper is the early straight-leg version, and is wearing a vintage handmade dress inspired by Barbie doll's Mattel-made dress. Barbie is marked "BARBIE®/PATS.PEND./©MCMLVIII/BY/MATTEL/INC." on her buttocks. Skipper is marked "SKIPPER/©1963/MATTEL INC." on her buttocks. Titian ponytail Barbie with dress: **$200.00 – 250.00.** Titian Skipper with dress: **$40.00 – 55.00.**

Japanese Skipper: These three straight-leg Skipper dolls were made for the Japanese market. They were issued in brunette, blond, and red hair. The Japanese Skipper dolls have black eyes, unlike the American Skipper who has blue eyes. The Japanese black-eyed Skippers look in the opposite direction than the American blue-eyed Skipper. The Japanese Skippers also have darker eyebrows than the American Skippers. Japanese Skippers without fashions: **$125.00 – 175.00.** *Courtesy Jennie Brott.*

Skipper: In 1965 Skipper dolls were made with bendable legs. By 1968 Skipper not only had bendable legs, but a Twist 'N Turn waist and rooted eyelashes as well. Here is a bend leg, Twist 'N Turn Skipper with rooted eyelashes. She is marked "©1967/Mattel, Inc/U.S. Pats. Pend./Made In Japan." on her buttocks. She is wearing one of her mod fashions called Hearts 'n Flowers. Doll without fashion: **$35.00 – 45.00.** Outfit good condition, near complete: **$55.00 – 75.00.**

Francie: Barbie's "MODern" cousin Francie is 10¾" and has a body which is shaped differently than Barbie doll's so that the two dolls couldn't share clothing very effectively. Naturally, a whole line of Francie clothing was produced by Mattel for the smaller-sized doll. Like many of the dolls in the Barbie line, Francie came in a number of different versions. The doll in the photo is a short haired Francie with a Twist 'N Turn waist and bendable legs. She is wearing a Mattel dress called Twigster. Francie is marked "©1965/MATTEL, INC./U.S. PATENTED/U.S. PAT.PEND./MADE IN/JAPAN." Doll with dress: **$85.00 – 100.00.**

Black Francie: Shown in the photo is a second issue black Francie doll from 1968 wearing Partners in Print, a Sears exclusive outfit sold separately for her. The hair on the 1968 black Francie dolls doesn't tend to oxidize like that on the first issue dolls, so it is usually a dark brunette color. The eyes on the second issue dolls are darker brown then the first issue. Loose doll without outfit: **$500.00. – 700.00.** Outfit alone, mint/complete: **$95.00 – 145.00.** *Courtesy Jennie Brott.*

Black Francie: Francie was the first doll in the Barbie line that Mattel issued in an African-American version. The doll was issued in 1967 and 1968. In the photo is a first version of black Francie that came out in 1967. The first version dolls have hair that often oxidizes to a reddish color and the eyes are rust color. At the time the black Francie was issued she was not very successful and relatively few numbers of the doll were sold. Consequently, today she is hard to find and extremely popular with Barbie collectors. MIB minus wrist tag and cellophane on box: **$2,000.00 – 2,500.00.**

Francie with Growin' Pretty Hair: This doll had a section of hair coming out of a hole in the back of her head that "grew" longer when tugged on lightly. Two different versions of Francie with Growin' Pretty Hair were issued. In 1970 she came in a cardboard box with a picture of the doll on the front. The doll itself couldn't be seen from inside the box. The arms of the 1970 Francie with Growin' Pretty Hair were the same as those on the Twist-N-Turn Barbie. The following year in addition to the 1970 version still being available, a second version of the doll was sold. The 1971 version shown in the photo came in a window box and now she also came with two hairpieces, unlike the earlier doll. The 1971 Francie with Growin' Pretty Hair had curved upwards arms made from what is known as the "Mexico" arm molds, the same used on Talking Barbie. 1972 window box version NRFB: **$225.00 – 300.00.**

Japanese Francie: These two Francie dolls were made for the Japanese market. The doll on the left is a straight-leg Japanese Francie with blue eyes wearing the dress, vest, and shoes to Twilight Twinkle from 1971. In the U.S. Francie was only issued with brown eyes, but in Japan she came with either blue or brown eyes. On the right is a Japanese Hair Happenin's Francie. She is the same as the American issued Hair Happenin's Francie doll. She is wearing the dress to Floating-In with replaced shoes. Japanese straight-leg Francie: **$500.00 – 800.00.** Twilight Twinkle dress, vest, shoes: **$125.00 – 200.00.** Japanese Hair Happenin's Francie: **$150.00 – 175.00.** Floating-in dress: **$40.00 – 50.00.** *Courtesy Jennie Brott.*

Casey: 10¾" Casey is the same size and has the same body as Francie so the two could share clothing. She has rooted eyelashes and came in blond or brunette. Some of the brunette dolls have hair that oxidized to a brassy or bright red color like the hair on the doll in the photo. The red-haired dolls are quite desirable to collectors as they are not common. Casey originally came with an earring in her left ear. The metal from the earring often turns the vinyl around the ear green if the earring has been left in over time. When this has happened, the doll's value decreases quite a bit. Casey is marked "©1966/ MATTEL, INC./U.S.PATENTED/U.S.PAT. PEND./MADE IN/JAPAN" on her buttocks. The doll in the photograph is wearing an outfit called Border-Line. Loose doll with red hair: **$145.00 – 200.00.** Outfit: **$40.00 – 65.00.**

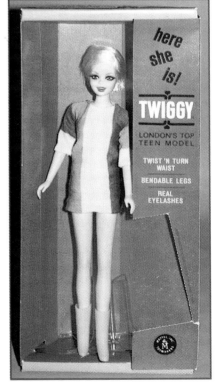

Twiggy: British fashion model Twiggy was made into a Barbie-sized doll. She was 10¾", the same size as Barbie's cousin Francie and was able to share clothing with Francie and Casey. In addition, Mattel made some clothing especially for Twiggy and gave them names like Twiggy-Do's, Twiggy Turnouts, Twigster, and Twiggy Gear. Twiggy is marked "©1966/MATTEL INC./U.S.PAT.PEND./ MADE IN/JAPAN" on her buttocks. Mint with box: **$250.00 – 300.00.** *Courtesy Robin Englehart, vintagelane.com, photos by Nancy Jean Mong.*

Twiggy: Twiggy shown with the back of her box.
Courtesy Robin Englehart, vintagelane.com, photos by Nancy Jean Mong.

Twiggy and Casey: Twiggy and Casey were made with the same head mold and are very similar in appearance. Twiggy has eyeliner all around her eyes which Casey does not and their hair color and styles are slightly different. Both dolls have the same markings. Shown in the photo are Twiggy on the left and a blond Casey on the right. Twiggy (wearing all original clothing): **$85.00 – 150.00.** Casey (dressed in authentic Francie/Casey clothing): **$75.00 – 100.00.**

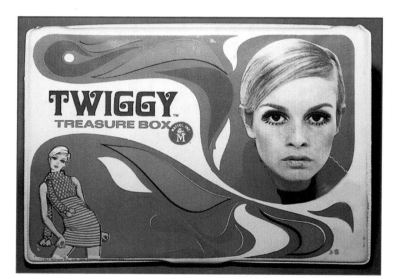

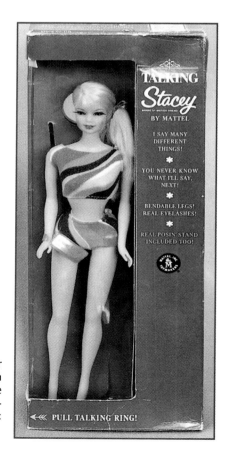

Twiggy Treasure Box: This treasure box by Mattel shows a photo of the real Twiggy, model Leslie Hornby, along with an illustration of the Twiggy doll wearing her Twigster outfit. The box is made of vinyl similar to many of Mattel's dolls carrying cases. **$35.00 – 65.00.** *Courtesy Robin Englehart, vintagelane.com, photos by Nancy Jean Mong.*

Talking Stacey: Talking Stacey has rooted eyelashes and came with red or platinum blond hair. She has speaker holes on her back and a pull-string in the back of her neck that activates the talking mechanism in her torso. She was available from 1968 to 1970. Talking Stacey is marked "©1967/MATTEL, INC./U.S. & FOREIGN/PATS.PEND./MEXICO." Mint with box/talking: **$225.00 – 300.00.**

Francie's fashions fit Casey. Barbie shares her clothes with Stacey and Christie. Dolls not included.

The Mod Look for Francie .. a Sears exclusive

5-piece Outfit $2.49

1 Orange Zip. Day coat with the look of leather. Dress has matching orange skirt and a striped knit top. With hanger, shoes. Shpg. wt. 7 oz.
49 N 30091 .. $2.49

Francie Outfits with slippers

2 Slumber Number. Nylon nightgown with a sleep shade. Shpg. wt. 4 oz.
49 N 34351 .. $1.29

3 Hill-Riders. Ribbed knit sweater and rayon slacks. Wt. 6 oz.
49 N 30098 .. $1.99

4 Night Blooms. Filmy negligee and gown. Wt. 7 oz.
49 N 34321 .. $2.69

Glimmer Glamour
A Sears exclusive $2.97

Fashion Favorites for Barbie and Stacey

5 Sparkly blue dress and fully-lined lamé coat. Gold-color hose, clear shoes. Hanger.
49 N 30089—Shipping weight 8 ounces. $2.97

6 Knit Hit. Dress in two colors with accent on the top. Hanger and footwear included.
49 N 34371—Shipping weight 5 ounces. $1.49

7 Trailblazers. A corduroy pantsuit with blouse and sunglasses. Hanger and shoes included.
49 N 30104—Shipping weight 7 ounces...$2.69

8 Wedding Wonder with train, ribbons and flowers. Satin slip, sheer veil. Hanger, shoes.
49 N 34387—Shipping weight 10 ounces.. $2.99

9 Jump into Lace. Elegant hostess pajamas. Plastic hanger and shoes included.
49 N 34375-Shipping weight 6 ounces....$1.97

Francie and Barbie have Twist 'n Turn waists $2.99 each

10 Francie with a striped knit swimsuit and long, bouncy rooted hair. Plastic stand included. Vinyl, 11½ in. tall with bendable legs, "real" lashes.
49 N 3550—Shpg. wt. 11 oz. $2.99

11 Barbie in a luscious swimsuit. Long, rooted hair. Plastic stand. Vinyl, 11½ in. tall with bendable legs.
49 N 3549—Shpg. wt. 11 oz. $2.99

Barbie, Stacey and Christie TALK $4.44 each

"Stacey and I are having tea"   "Let's have Barbie over for tea"   "Let's visit Barbie and Stacey"

(12 thru 14) Listen in on the gabfest. Each doll says many full-length, teen phrases .. all at random. Stacey has a British accent. Just pull the talking ring, no batteries needed. Clear stand combines with box cap to form a chair. Vinyl dolls are 11½ in. tall. Rooted hair, "real" lashes and bendable legs. Shipping weight each 12 ounces.
(12) 49 N 30015—Talking Barbie......... $4.44
(13) 49 N 30014—Talking Stacey......... 4.44
(14) 49 N 30072—Talking Christie....... 4.44

STRIPES are happening

Only Sears combines this super new outfit with

Twist 'n Turn Stacey

8-piece Gift Set $5.97

Stacey loves this madly mod sports ensemble. Wide striped shell, skirt and socks. Jacket top and matching ankle boots. Vinyl, 11½-in. Stacey doll has twist 'n turn waist and bendable legs. Rooted hair, "real" eyelashes. Clothes hanger and a clear plastic posing stand included. Stacey comes dressed in a fashionable 1-piece swimsuit.
49 N 30087—Shipping wt. 1 lb...........$5.97

NOTE, both pages: Doll clothing from Japan.   PGDL   Sears 601

Barbie and Friends: This page from the Sears 1968 Christmas catalog shows some of the Barbie and friends dolls and outfits available that year, including three Sears exclusive outfits, Glimmer Glamour for Barbie, Orange Zip for Francie, and a Stripes Are Happening Stacey gift set. *Sears 1968 Christmas Catalog.*

Julia: Representing the nurse played by Diahann Carroll in the television series *Julia*, a Barbie-sized doll called Julia was produced by Mattel starting in 1969. Mattel's Julia doll used the face mold from their earlier Christie dolls. Julia also had the same body as Mattel's Twist 'N Turn Barbie, allowing her to share Barbie's clothing and vice versa. Julia came in a Twist 'N Turn or talking version. The Twist 'N Turn Julia shown in the photo is wearing Talking Julia's original jumpsuit. Julia is marked "©1966/MATTEL, INC./U.S. PATENTED/U.S. PAT.PEND./MADE IN/JAPAN" on her buttocks. Loose doll redressed in vintage fashion: **$65.00 – 95.00.** *Courtesy Robin Englehart, vintagelane.com, photos by Nancy Jean Mong.*

Tutti and Todd: These 6½" dolls were Barbie doll's little sister Tutti and her twin brother Todd. Standard Tutti dolls came in either blond or brunette hair. Dolls were also issued in red (called titian) or black hair, but these hair colors were usually reserved for dolls that came in special gift sets and the hair was usually styled differently than the standard dolls. Most Todd dolls have titian hair, but some Todd dolls can be found with brunette hair. Both Tutti and Todd were made with the same body mold and have wires inside their arms and legs allowing them to be posed. It's not uncommon to find these wires have broken from overuse or have chemically reacted over the years with the vinyl surrounding it, leaving green stains on the doll and devaluing it. Tutti is much easier to locate than her twin brother as she was available for a longer period of time. Tutti and Todd were reissued and sold in Europe for many years after they were discontinued in the United States. Tutti and Todd are marked "©1965/MATTEL, INC./JAPAN" on their backs. Tutti: **$30.00 – 50.00.** Todd: **$45.00 – 75.00.**

Chris: One of Tutti's 6½" friends was Chris. She came with blond or brunette hair that sometimes oxidized to an auburn or red color. Two green hair ribbons tied in bows held small sections of her long hair on the sides of her head. A small green barrette was also in her hair on one side. Chris is marked "©1965/MATTEL, INC./JAPAN" on her back. MIB: **$100.00 – 200.00.**

Pos 'n Play Tiff: Skipper-sized Tiff was available in 1972. She was made from the same mold as Mattel's Fluff doll. Tiff has titian hair and brown eyes. She has jointed wrists, ball-jointed shoulders, and bendable elbows and knees. Her shirt has a "STOP" sticker on the front and she has "HELP!" and "GO!" stickers on her dungaree slacks. These stickers often fell off the clothing over the years so it is hard to find them on a loose doll. Tiff came with her own skateboard to ride. She is marked "©1969 MATTEL, INC./TAIWAN/U.S. & FOR. PATD./OTHER PATS.PEND/PATD IN CANADA 1967" on her buttocks. She is extremely hard to find as she was available for only a short period of time. Loose and all original with wrist tag and skateboard: **$185.00 – 220.00.**

Walk Lively Miss America: 11½" Miss America had a head that turned, and arms and legs that moved in a "walking" action. She had rooted eyelashes and brunette or blond curly hair. The doll was available beginning in 1972. She was not only sold in stores but was available through a Kellogg Company mail-away promotional for two Corn Flakes box tops and three dollars in cash. Miss America is marked "©1967 MATTEL INC./U.S. PAT. PEND./TAIWAN" on her buttocks. The doll in the photo is wearing her complete outfit with the accessories she came with. Loose doll/complete: **$75.00 – 90.00.**

Chatty Cathy: Chatty Cathy talked with the use of a pull-string on the back of her neck. Many variations of Chatty Cathy dolls were produced by Mattel. Variations include the length and style of hair, eye color, positioning of fingers, shape of the speaker grill on the stomach, whether the vinyl on the doll's head is soft or hard, and lots of other little subtle characteristics resulting in a large variety of Chatty Cathy dolls for the collector. Here are many examples of different dolls and outfits that Chatty Cathy either came in or which were sold separately. While most Chatty Cathy dolls are marked the first issue doll bears no markings. The standard Chatty Cathy dolls are marked "CHATTY CATHY™/PATENTS PENDING/©MCMLX/ BY MATTEL, INC./HAWTHORNE, CALIF." on their backs. The pigtailed Chatty Cathy dolls are marked "CHATTY CATHY®/©1960/CHATTY BABY™/©1961/ BY MATTEL, INC./U.S.PAT. 3,017,187/OTHER U.S. &/FOREIGN PATS. PEND./PAT'D IN CANADA 1962" on their backs. Original Chatty clothing adds quite a bit to the value, so when Chatty dolls are not wearing either their original clothes or any Chatty clothing, the value is approximately half of book value. With original or tagged Chatty clothing: **$85.00 – 300.00,** on the lower end if mute, higher end if talking. *Courtesy Mark A. Salyers.*

Chatty Cathy: Chatty Cathy with pigtails wearing her #697 Playtime outfit which was sold separately. Chatty Cathy dolls with pigtails are less common than dolls with shoulder-length hair. Pigtailed Chatty dolls will have a definite part in the back of their hair so if the hair is down, you can determine if it's a pigtailed doll by looking for the part. The pigtailed dolls come in blond, brunette, or red hair. Chatty collectors refer to these pigtailed dolls as "piggys." Chatty Cathy with pigtails, talking, and wearing Playtime outfit: **$145.00 – 225.00.**

Singin' Chatty: Singin' Chatty sang songs when her "chatty" ring was pulled. She was issued with blond or brunette hair. The two Singin' Chatty dolls in the photo are modeling two of the three variations of her original dress. The dolls are marked "SINGIN' CHATTY™/©1964 MATTEL, INC./HAWTHORNE, CALIF., USA/PATENTED IN USA /PATENTED IN CANADA 1962/OTHER PATENTS PENDING" on their bodies. **$35.00 – 65.00.** *Courtesy Mark A. Salyers.*

Chatty Baby: In 1962 Chatty Cathy received an 18" little sister, Chatty Baby. Chatty Baby came with either blond or brunette hair. She is marked "CHATTY CATHY®/©1960/CHATTY BABY™/©1961/ BY MATTEL, INC./U.S.PAT. 3,017,187/OTHER U.S. &/FOREIGN PATS. PEND./PAT'D IN CANADA 1962." With original clothing: **$65.00 – 90.00,** on the lower end if mute, higher end if talking.

Chatty Baby: In 1970 – 1971 a restyled Chatty Baby was issued. She bore little resemblance to the earlier Chatty Baby. Shown in the photo is the reissued Chatty Baby with her original box. The reissued Chatty Baby is marked "©1969 MATTEL, INC./MEXICO" on her head and "©1964 MATTEL, INC./HAWTHORNE, CALIF., USA/ PATENTED IN USA/PATENTED IN CANADA 1962/OTHER PATENTS PENDING/MADE IN MEXICO" on her body. MIB: **$65.00 – 85.00.** *Courtesy Mark A. Salyers.*

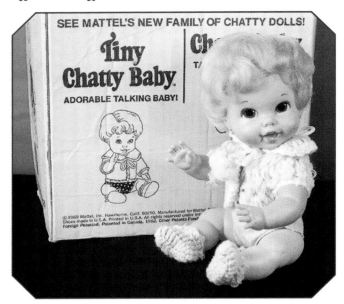

Tiny Chatty Baby: In 1970 – 1971 Tiny Chatty Baby was also reissued. The reissued Tiny Chatty Baby was basically the same doll as Mattel's Baby Small Talk, only Tiny Chatty Baby had brown eyes instead of blue and her body was marked "Mexico" instead of "Hong Kong." Tiny Chatty Baby is marked "©1967 MATTEL, INC./HONG KONG" on her head and "©1967 MATTEL, INC./U.S. & FOR./PATS. PEND./MEXICO" on her body. The Tiny Chatty Baby in the photo is shown with the back of Chatty Baby's box. Loose doll: **$25.00 – 35.00.** *Courtesy Mark A. Salyers.*

Talking Bozo: 18" pull-string Talking Bozo doll. Mattel made other size Bozo dolls as well and several different Bozo puppets. Mute: **$35.00 – 45.00.** Talking: **$45.00 – 85.00.** *Courtesy Robin Englehart, vintagelane.com, photos by Nancy Jean Mong.*

Scooba-Doo: A Beatnik-type pull-string talking doll with a vinyl head and plush body and limbs. She has heavy eye makeup around her open and close eyes. When her eyes are shut her most unusual black eyelids can be seen. Her striped dress is removable but the black stockings and shirt are part of her stuffed body. She comes with a chain necklace. The 22" doll was issued in either black or platinum hair. Her beatnik phrases include "Play it cool, don't be a square," "Hey doll, like you're way out there," "I'm hip like ya know, a beatnik," "Hey sweetie, like you're something else ya know," "I dig that crazy beat, yah," "Dig my crazy black stockings," "I dig food, like when do we eat?" "Come on let's get with it, like weeee!," and she sings two different scat style scooba-doo-ba songs. Scooba-Doo is unmarked on her head. Her body is tagged, "QUALITY ORIGINALS BY/MATTEL®/SCOO-BA-Doo™, ©1964 Mattel, Inc./Hawthorne, Calif./Made in U.S.A./U.S. Pats. 3,017,187, 8,082,006 & 3,095,201/Pat'd. in Canada 1962, Other Pats. Pend." Back of tag gives material content. The platinum blond Scooba-Doo in the photo is wearing her original dress but is missing her chain necklace. Loose and talking: **$75.00 – 95.00.** *Courtesy Lisa Petrucci.*

Scooba-Doo: A black-haired Scooba-Doo showing her heavy eye makeup. Loose and talking: **$75.00 – 95.00.**

Dee-Dee: 15" doll with a cut 'n button fashion wardrobe. Young children could just cut out the pre-printed fabric then button the pieces together. The four outfits included a nightgown, a coat, an A-line dress, and a swimsuit. Dee-Dee is made of a high-quality heavy vinyl. She is marked "Made in Japan/©1964 Mattel, Inc./Hawthorne, Calif. USA" on her body. She is shown wearing the dress she was sold in, along with the original insert from her box. Mint/complete: **$75.00 – 85.00.** *Courtesy Mark A. Salyers.*

Dee-Dee: 15" Dee-Dee wearing her original dress and shoes, with replaced socks. Loose doll: **$25.00 – 40.00.**

Baby First Step (1965): This 18" battery-operated doll was issued starting in 1965. The photo shows the first issue Baby First Step with her original box and roller-skates. The doll is marked "©1964 MATTEL, INC./HAWTHORNE, CALIFORNIA/MADE IN U.S.A./U.S. PATENTS PENDING" on her back. MIB/working: **$125.00 – 145.00.**

Baby First Step (1965): Baby First Step on the right in the photo is shown wearing the usual dress most first issue Baby First Steps are found in. The doll on the left is wearing an unusual variation of this dress. MIB/working: **$125.00 – 145.00.** Loose doll/working: **$40.00 – 55.00.** *Courtesy Mark A. Salyers.*

Talking Baby First Step (1966): In 1966 Baby First Step was also issued in a talking version. Like Baby First Step, Talking Baby First Step was battery operated so she could walk and roller skate. In addition she had a pull string to make her talk. Talking Baby First Step is marked "©1964 MATTEL INC./HAWTHORNE, CALIFORNIA/MADE IN USA/U.S. PATENTS PENDING" on her body. MIB/working: **$75.00 – 95.00.** *Courtesy Mark A. Salyers.*

Baby First Step and Talking Baby First Step: Although their faces are similar, Talking Baby First Step's head is much larger than Baby First Step's.

Baby First Step (1967): In 1967 Baby First Step came issued in an updated, more mod flower and polka-dot print dress. Her hair is slightly longer than the earlier issued doll. The second issue doll is marked "©1964 MATTEL INC./HAWTHORNE, CALIFORNIA/ MADE IN USA/U.S. PATENTS PENDING" on her head. MIB/working: **$100.00 – 125.00.** *Courtesy Mark A. Salyers.*

Talking Baby First Step (1967): In 1967 Talking Baby First Step was also issued in an updated, more modern dress. Talking Baby First Step is marked "©1967 MATTEL, INC./U.S. & FOR. PATS. PEND." on her head and "©1964 MATTEL INC./ HAWTHORNE, CALIFOR-NIA/MADE IN USA/U.S. PATENTS PENDING" on her body. Working: **$45.00 – 60.00.** *Courtesy Mark A. Salyers.*

Baby First Step (1968): In 1968 Mattel issued a restyled "new" Baby First Step with a smiling, friendlier face. The 19" Baby First Step was about an inch taller than the 1964 issue. The new Baby First Step is marked "©1967 MATTEL, INC. U.S.A./U.S. & FOR. PATS. PEND." on her head and "©1964 MATTEL, INC./HAWTHORNE, CALIFORNIA/MADE IN U.S.A./U.S. PATENTS PENDING" on her back. Doll with original box, skates, and hang-tag/working: **$75.00 – 100.00.** *Courtesy Mark A. Salyers.*

133

Baby First Step (1968): Another example of the restyled Baby First Step. Doll with original box/working: **$65.00 – 80.00.**

Talking Baby First Step (1968): Talking Baby First Step with the new restyled smiling face. Talking Baby First Step is marked "©1967 MATTEL, INC./ U.S. & FOR. PATS. PEND." on her head, and "©1964 MATTEL INC./ HAWTHORNE, CALIFORNIA / MADE IN USA / U.S. PATENTS PENDING" on her body. Working: **$45.00 – 55.00.** *Courtesy Mark A. Salyers.*

Baby First Step: This Baby First Step was made for the U.K. market by Rosebud. Her markings are the same as the 1965 and 1966 American versions of Baby First Step, "©1964 MATTEL INC./ HAWTHORNE, CALIFOR-NIA/MADE IN USA/U.S. PATENTS PENDING" on her back. She has open and shut eyes, unlike the American dolls who have painted eyes. The British doll's arms and head are made from a rubbery kind of plastic rather than the harder vinyl used on the American dolls. MIB: **$250.00 – 350.00.** *Courtesy Mark A. Salyers.*

Babystep (1967 – 1968): Babystep was a Sears exclusive. In 1967 she had auburn hair and came wearing a red and blue outfit. In 1968 she came with blond hair and was sold wearing a yellow and blue outfit. Babystep is marked "©1964 MATTEL INC./ HAWTHORNE, CALIFORNIA/MADE IN USA/U.S. PATENTS PENDING" on her body. Loose and working: **$35.00 – 55.00.** Mint with box/working: **$85.00 – 110.00.** *Courtesy Mark A. Salyers.*

Baby Walk 'N See (1967): Another Sears exclusive doll available in 1967. Baby Walk 'n See had look-around eyes that moved when she walked. She is marked "©1966 Mattel Inc., USA/U.S. Patent Pending" on her head and "©1964 Mattel Inc./Hawthorne, California/Made in USA/U.S. Patents Pending" on her body. MIB with hang-tag/working: **$100.00 – 125.00.** *Courtesy Mark A. Salyers.*

Baby's Hungry!: Available 1967 only, 17½" Baby's Hungry! moves her mouth and lips and rolls her eyes as she chews her food and drinks from her bottle. Her Feed and Carry Chair was a Sears exclusive in 1967. When opened, the carrying case doubled as a feeding chair with a tray and overhead awning. Baby's Hungry! is marked "©1966 Mattel Inc. USA/U.S. Patents Pending/4" on her head and "©1966 Mattel, Inc/ Hawthorne, California/U.S. Pats. Pend.-Made in USA" on her body. Doll with Feed and Carry Chair: **$55.00 – 85.00.** *Courtesy Mark A. Salyers.*

1967 Baby Say 'N See: 16½" pull-string talker has eyes and mouth that move when she speaks. Baby Say 'N See says things like "I have beautiful eyes 'cause I eat carrots" and "Can you make your eyes go 'round and 'round like this?" The doll is marked "©1966 Mattel Inc. U.S.A./U.S. Patent Pending" on her head, and tagged "Quality Originals by Mattel®/BABY SAY 'N SEE™/©1965 Mattel, Inc./Hawthorne, Calif./Sewn body/made in Japan/Pat'd in U.S.A./Other Pats. Pend." on her body. Missing original clothing/talking: **$35.00 – 45.00.**

Little Sister Look & Say: A pull-string talking Sears exclusive doll available in 1967 and 1968. In Sears catalogs she was advertised as being "Sister Look 'n Say" in 1967 with a small "n," and "Sister Look 'N Say" with a capital "N" in 1968, however, the doll itself is tagged "Little Sister Look & Say." The doll is marked "©1966 Mattel Inc., USA/U.S. Patent Pending" on her head, and tagged "Quality Originals by Mattel®/Little Sister Look & Say /©1966 Mattel, Inc./ Hawthorne, Calif./Sewn body made in Hong Kong/ Pat'd in USA/Pat'd Canada 1962/ Other Pats. Pend." on her body. Talking: **$35.00 – 45.00.** *Courtesy Mark A. Salyers.*

Baby Small Talk: a 10" pull-string talking doll. Baby Small Talk is marked "©1967 MATTEL INC./HONG KONG" on her head and "©1967 MATTEL. INC./U.S. & FOR. PATS. PEND./HONG KONG" on her back. The doll in the photo is shown in her original box. The side flaps of the box have been pulled forward for the photo to show the illustrations of the doll. Mattel used the Small Talk face mold for many other dolls. MIB/talking: **$75.00 – 95.00.** *Courtesy Robin Englehart, vintagelane.com, photo by Nancy Jean Mong.*

Baby Small Talk: A rare NRFB black Baby Small Talk is shown next to a loose white version of the doll. MIB black doll/talking: **$75.00 – 125.00.** Loose, white/talking: **$25.00 – 40.00.** *Courtesy Kathleen Tornikoski, Romancing the Doll.*

Baby Small Walk: A 10" battery-operated walking doll. The doll is marked "©1967 MATTEL INC./16" on her head and "©1967 MATTEL. INC./U.S. & FOREIGN PATENTS PENDING/U.S.A" on her back. This doll could be purchased alone or in a set with her Scootabout and Happy Horsy like the one shown here. MIB with accessories/working: **$85.00 – 100.00.** *Courtesy Robin Englehart, vintagelane.com, photo by Nancy Jean Mong.*

137

Sister Small Talk: 10" pull-string talking doll shown in her original box. She is marked, "©1967 MATTEL INC. JAPAN" on her head and "©1967 MATTEL INC./U.S. & FOR./PATS PEND./U.S.A" on her back. With original box/talking: **$50.00 – 65.00.**

Talkin' Twins Trish: 11" Trish has blond hair. She wears a striped top with a yellow leather skirt and white boots. She is marked "©1967 Mattel Inc./Japan" on her head. Her body is tagged "Quality Originals by Mattel®/Talkin' Twins™/©1970 Mattel, Inc./Hawthorne, Calif./Made in Hong Kong/ALL NEW MATERIALS/Consisting of: Shredded Clippings 90%/Polyurethane Foam 10%/U.S. and Foreign Pat'd/Other Patents Pending." Loose doll/talking: **$35.00 – 45.00.** Loose/mute: **$20.00 – 30.00.**

Talkin' Twins Tracy: This 11" pull-string talking doll uses the Baby Small Talk or Baby Small Walk head on a stuffed cloth body. Her original box calls her "A Pretty Talk Doll" while her tag refers to her as one of the "Talkin' Twins." Tracy has auburn hair, a flowered top, a green leather skirt, green leather boots, and a matching removable green vest which very often is missing on loose dolls. She is marked "©1967 Mattel Inc./Hong Kong" on her head. Her body is tagged "Quality Originals by Mattel®/Talkin' Twins™/©1970 Mattel, Inc./Hawthorne, Calif./Made in Hong Kong/ALL NEW MATERIALS/Consisting of: Shredded Clippings 90%/Polyurethane Foam 10%/US and Foreign Pat'd/Other Patents Pending." MIB/talking: **$75.00 – 95.00.**

Small Talk Cheerleader: The actual name of these pull-string talking cheerleader dolls that use the Baby Small Walk head on a stuffed cloth body is unknown, since the author has yet to see one in its box or find any type of advertisement for them. Many different cheerleader dolls representing various state universities have been spotted by collectors. Some cheerleaders have letters on the front of their outfits such as "A" for Arkansas or "O" for Oklahoma, while others have been found with no letter on the front. Here the 13½" Oklahoma cheerleader is shown with Talkin' Twins Tracey. The clothing on the cheerleader dolls is not removable. Cheerleader/talking: **$30.00 – 35.00.** Cheerleader/mute: **$15.00 – 20.00.** *Courtesy Sharon Wendrow, Memory Lane.*

Small Talk Cheerleader: Another 13½" talking Cheerleader from Arkansas. Talking: **$30.00 – 35.00.** Mute: **$15.00 – 20.00.** *Courtesy Rebecca Sevrin.*

Storybook Small Talk, Talking Goldilocks: Two different pull-string Talking Goldilocks dolls with the Small Talk face. The doll on the left has long straight bright blond hair. She is marked "©1967 MATTEL INC./HONG KONG" on her head and "©1967 MATTEL. INC./U.S. & FOR. PATS. PEND./HONG KONG" on her back. The doll on the right has golden blond hair that is shorter and curlier than the doll on the left. She is marked "©1967 MATTEL INC. JAPAN" on her head and "©1967 MATTEL. INC./U.S. & FOR./PATS. PEND./MEXICO" on her back. Loose doll/working: **$30.00 – 55.00.** In original box/working: **$85.00 – 100.00.**

Baby Walk 'N Play: 11¾" battery-operated doll from 1970 came with a set of toys to play with as she walks along. Baby Walk 'N Play is marked "©1967 Mattel Inc./Hong Kong" on her head and "©1967 Mattel, Inc./U.S. & Foreign Patented/Other Patents Pending/Hong Kong" on her body. Like many other Mattel dolls she has the Small Talk face. MIB/working: **$75.00 – 100.00.** *Courtesy Mark A. Salyers.*

Tippee Toes: Tippee Toes is a battery-operated doll whose legs move allowing her to ride her tricycle or horse. 16" Tippee Toes is marked "JAPAN" on her head and "©1967 MATTEL, INC./HAWTHORNE, CALIFORNIA/MADE IN U.S.A." on her back. Tippee Toes' blue plastic tricycle with yellow plastic wheels is marked "©1967 MATTEL, INC./HAWTHORNE, CALIFORNIA/U.S. PATENT PENDING/MADE IN U.S.A." The yellow horse with pink details and green wheels is marked "©1967 MATTEL, INC. HAWTHORNE, CALIF. MADE IN U.S.A." With box and accessories/working: **$125.00 – 145.00.** *Courtesy Robin Englehart, vintagelane.com, photos by Nancy Jean Mong.*

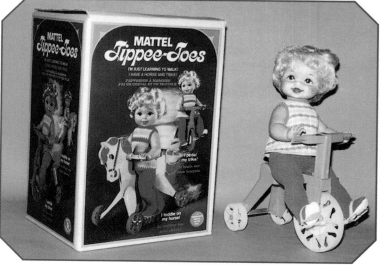

140

Tippee Toes/Coki: Here is an Italian version of Tippee Toes, named Coki. She was made by Ratti-Mattel for the Italian market. Like the American version she comes with a horse and tricycle. She has open and shut eyes, unlike the American version who has painted eyes. Coki is marked "Italy" on her head and "©1967 MATTEL, INC./ HAWTHORNE, CALIF./MADE IN USA" on her body. Italian Coki with box: **$300.00 – 400.00.** *Courtesy Mark A. Salyers.*

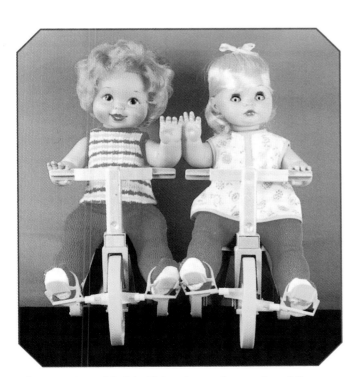

Tippee Toes/Coki: This photo shows the difference between the American and Italian versions of Tippee Toes and Coki. *Courtesy Mark A. Salyers.*

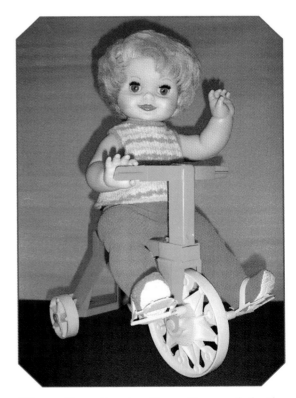

Tippee Toes: Here is a Tippee Toes made for the U.K. market. It is unknown if she was sold under a different name than the American-issued Tippee Toes. She has open and shut eyes. She is marked "©1967 MATTEL, INC./HAWTHORNE, CALIF./MADE IN USA." U.K. doll with tricycle: **$100.00 – 135.00.** *Courtesy Mark A. Salyers.*

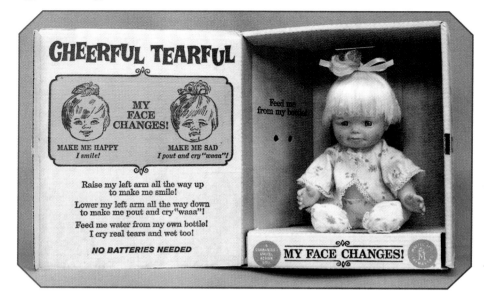

Cheerful Tearful: This 13" doll pouts when her arm is raised and lowered and she cries "real" tears. She is shown with her original box. Cheerful Tearful is marked "©1965 MATTEL, INC./ HAWTHORNE, CALIF./ U.S.PATENTS/ PEND-ING/3036-014-3" on her back. MIB: **$100.00 – 150.00.**

Randi Reader: 18" battery-operated doll who reads out loud. Her eyes move as she talks and reads the storybook you place in her hands. She says 15 different phrases when you raise her arm. Randi is marked "©1967 MATTEL INC./ U.S. & FOR. PATS. PEND./U.S.A." on her back. Her dress is tagged "RANDI®Reader/©1967 MATTEL. INC./MEXICO." Mint doll with original hang tag/working: **$35.00 – 45.00.**

Randi Reader: Shown with her original box, plastic story card, and storybook. MIB with accessories/working: **$50.00 – 75.00.** *Courtesy Mark A. Salyers.*

Swingy: This battery-operated 18" doll swings back and forth as if dancing. She came in white or a rare black version like the doll shown here. Swingy came with a cardboard 33⅓ rpm record to dance to. The doll is marked "©1967 MATTEL, INC./U.S. & FOR. PATS. PEND" on her head and "©1964 MATTEL, INC./HAWTHORNE, CAL/MADE IN USA./U.S. & FOREIGN PATENTED/OTHER PATENTS PENDING" on her back. Black Swingy/working: **$45.00 – 65.00.** *Courtesy Mark A. Salyers.*

Swingy: White and black Swingy dolls wearing their original pink polka dot dresses are shown with a Swingy in the center wearing a different original dress. White Swingy/working: **$35.00 – 50.00.** Black Swingy/working: **$45.00 – 65.00.** *Courtesy Mark A. Salyers.*

Tiny Swingy: This 11" battery-operated version of Swingy uses the Small Talk face mold. She is shown with her original box and record. The doll is marked "©1967 MATTEL, INC./HONG KONG" on her head and "©1967 MATTEL, INC./ U.S. & FOREIGN PATENTED/OTHER PATENTS PENDING/HONG KONG" on her back. MIB/working: **$85.00 – 115.00.**
Courtesy Mark A. Salyers.

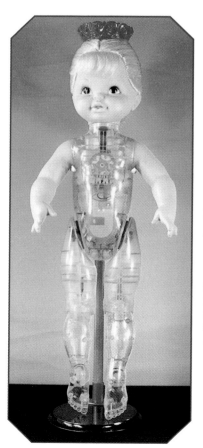

Prototype Dancerina: Here is an extremely rare prototype Dancerina showing the mechanics inside her clear plastic torso and legs. So far, only three of these prototypes are known to exist, but there could be more yet-to-be-discovered prototypes like this one hidden away somewhere. The prototype doll is marked "©1968 MATTEL, INC./MEXICO" on her head and "©1968 MATTEL, INC. / MADE IN USA / U.S. PATENT PENDING" on her body. Not enough examples available to determine a fair market value. *Courtesy Mark A. Salyers.*

Dancerina: Dancerina is a 24" battery-operated doll who dances when the center of her crown is pulled up or spins around when the center of her crown is pressed down. She originally came with a small size 33⅓ rpm record featuring ballet music. She came in a white or a hard-to-find black version as shown here. Dancerina is marked "©1968 MATTEL, INC. MEXICO" on her head and "©1968 MATTEL, INC./MADE IN U.S.A./U.S. PATENT PENDING" on her back. Black Dancerina/working: **$75.00 – 150.00.**
Courtesy Mark A. Salyers.

144

Danzerina: Here is an Italian version of Dancerina called Danzerina. The doll has open and shut eyes, although her original box shows the painted eye American version of Dancerina. The record that came with the Italian Danzerina doll is titled with the American spelling of Dancerina on it. MIB: **$400.00 – 500.00.** *Courtesy Robin Englehart, vintagelane.com, photo by Nancy Jean Mong.*

Baby Dancerina: Here is a smaller 11" version of Dancerina called Baby Dancerina. The doll came with a blue crown, a blue tutu, ballet slippers, and a 33⅓ rpm record to dance to. Baby Dancerina is marked "1969 MATTEL, INC./HONG KONG" on her head and "©1969 MATTEL, INC./U.S. & FOREIGN/PATENTS PENDING/HONG KONG" on her body. MIB w/record: **$45.00 – 65.00.** *Courtesy Mark A. Salyers.*

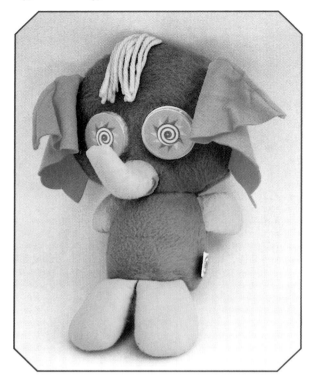

Googlie Elephant: Mattel's Googlie elephant from 1966 is 13" tall with a small amount of yarn hair on the top of his head and felt ears and a felt tongue. He has hypnotic eyes that spin, and he lets out a shrill squeal when you squeeze his belly. He is tagged "Quality Originals/by Mattel®/The Googlies ™/©1967 Mattel, Inc./Hawthorne, Calif./Made in Hong Kong." Other stuffed Googlies included an orange cat, a yellow bear, a blue dog, a pink rabbit, and a purple pig. They are not very common, but not a lot of collectors are actively looking for them, so they are still pretty affordable. **$35.00 – 40.00.** *Courtesy Jennie Brott.*

Off to See the Wizard Puppet: Pull-string talking puppet, featuring Dorothy, the Tin Man, the Scarecrow, and The Wizard of Oz, with the Cowardly Lion printed on the fabric portion of the puppet. NRFB: **$125.00 – 200.00.** *Courtesy Hillary and Cliff James, Toy With Me.*

Baby Fun: A 7¼" doll who came with a party noise maker, a horn, balloons, and a bubble pipe. Baby Fun is marked "©1968 MATTEL INC./ HONG/ KONG" on her head and "PATENT PENDING/ ©1968 MATTEL, INC./ HONG KONG" on her back. Circa 1973. MIB: **$50.00 – 60.00.**

146

Liddle Kiddles: Ranging in sizes from ¼" to 4" Mattel's Liddle Kiddles have rapidly appreciated in value in the past few years as more and more collectors have rediscovered these childhood favorites. The Liddle Kiddle line included over 100 dolls so only a small sampling is shown here. Values listed include the dolls' very small accessories. Because the tiny accessories so often got lost, in some cases they could be worth more than the dolls themselves. There really is no one formula for determining value of complete sets of Liddle Kiddles versus only the dolls. Some Kiddle dolls are relatively common, so they may be worth only about $15.00 by themselves. Add their original accessories and the value could shoot up to $60.00 or higher. It is common to find that over the years the vinyl on many Liddle Kiddles has turned green in places from the wires inside them. Even those dolls still on their original card or in their original packaging often turn green. In addition, the vinyl on Liddle Kiddles often discolors to a white, usually a result of being exposed to too much light. Values listed below are for Kiddles that do not have any discoloration. If any discoloration is on the doll, the value of that doll can be 50% lower than the values listed here.

The first series of Kiddles issued starting in 1966 included Babe Biddle, Bunson Burnie, Calamity Jiddle, Florence Niddle, Howard "Biff" Boodle, Greta Griddle, Liddle Diddle, Lola Liddle, and Millie Middle.

The second series of Kiddles issued starting in 1967 included Beddy Bye Biddle, Freezy Sliddle, Pretty Priddle, Rolly Twiddle, Sizzly Friddle, Soapy Siddle, Surfy Skiddle, Trikey Triddle, and Windy Fliddle.

The third series included Kampy Kiddle, Lemons Stiddle, Slipsy Sliddle, and Telly Viddle.

Beat-A-Diddle and Baby Liddle were Sears exclusive dolls. Beat-A-Diddle was available in 1966 and 1967 and Baby Liddle was available in 1968.

These 24 Kiddles are the most popular with collectors and when mint and complete their sets can run anywhere from $50.00 on up. Sears exclusive Liddle Kiddles can run over $200.00 for mint complete sets. Funny comic books came with all 24 of these Kiddles and a hair brush and comb were also included with many of them. Many people consider Kiddle sets complete even without the comb, brush, or comic that originally came with the dolls. Purists believe that if a Kiddle set is really considered to be complete, it should also include these three extra accessories. In this book, the values stated for complete sets do not include the comics or the hairbrush and comb. Kiddle comics usually run about $15.00 – 25.00 each and combs and brushes are usually valued at $1.00 – 3.00 each.

Liddle Kiddle dolls are marked with the company's name, "Mattel, Inc." or "M.I." on them. Many Liddle Kiddles were made in Japan and are marked so, however the smaller locket-size dolls are marked "Taiwan," and some of the jewelry-size dolls are marked "Hong Kong." Many competitors put out small dolls that looked very much like Mattel's Liddle Kiddles. Often when loose the dolls are thought to be Liddle Kiddles by those not thoroughly familiar with Kiddles. These imitation dolls, dubbed as "Kiddle Klones" by collectors, are often only marked "Hong Kong" or "Made in Hong Kong." The key to telling a real Kiddle from a knock-off one is the markings. If the doll does not carry the Mattel markings, it is likely it is an imitation doll and not a genuine Liddle Kiddle.

Babe Biddle: 3" Babe Biddle was one of the original nine Liddle Kiddles and like all the early Kiddles is now very popular with collectors. Babe's outfit consisted of a sleeveless one-piece playsuit with a blue skirt and blue and white gingham top, a red jacket with white vinyl collar, a blue hair scarf, and blue t-strap shoes. She came with a yellow car marked "Liddle Kiddle" on the trunk. The car has a clear plastic windshield which often is missing. Mint and complete set: **$60.00 – 85.00.**

Liddle Kiddles Type: Busy Bendees by S. Rosenberg Co. Inc. was one group of dolls that imitated many of Mattel's Liddle Kiddle dolls. Shown here is a Busy Bendee doll with many similarities to Babe Biddle. With case and accessories: **$15.00 – 25.00.** *Courtesy Robin Englehart, vintagelane.com, photo by Nancy Jean Mong.*

Sizzly Friddle: 3" Sizzly Friddle is shown on her original card. Liddle Kiddle collectors consider dolls like this as being mint-on-small-card, or MOSC. When still inside the blue card with the Liddle Kiddle title on it, it is considered mint-on-large-card or NRFP. MOSC: **$150.00 – 225.00.** *Courtesy Robin Englehart, vintagelane.com.*

Soapy Siddle: 3½" Soapy Siddle shown on her original small card. MOSC: **$150.00 – 225.00.** *Courtesy Robin Englehart, vintagelane.com.*

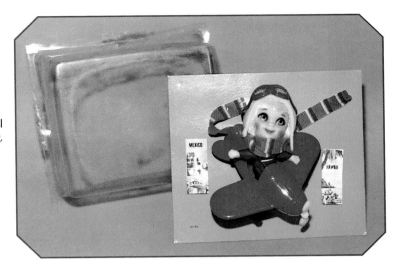

Windy Fliddle: 2⅞" Windy still on her original small card. MOSC: **$150.00 – 225.00.** *Courtesy Robin Englehart, vintagelane.com, photo by Nancy Jean Mong.*

Surfy Skiddle: A loose 3" Surfy Skiddle doll complete with all her accessories is shown with a mint-on-small-card Surfy. MOSC: **$150.00 – 225.00.** Loose/complete: **$95.00 – 125.00.** *Courtesy Robin Englehart, vintagelane.com, photo by Nancy Jean Mong.*

Kampy Kiddle: 3½" Kampy was a green-eyed camping Kiddle. Her hair was either bright blond or platinum and originally came in a ponytail with a mauve hair bow tied around it. She came dressed in a yellow sleeveless shirt and denim jeans. She was sold barefoot. Her accessories included a sleeping bag which originally had a "Kiddle Sleeping Bag" sticker on it (usually missing on loose sets), a fishing pole with green plastic fish, and a frying pan. Loose/complete: **$95.00 – 135.00.**

Kampy Kiddle: Kampy Kiddle shown NRFP with her original comic book. NRFP: **$375.00 – 425.00.** *Courtesy Robin Englehart, vintagelane.com, photo by Nancy Jean Mong.*

Rolly Twiddle and Lois Locket Kiddle: Mattel made only three different African American Liddle Kiddles: Rolly Twiddle, Lois Locket, and Baby Rockaway (not shown). On the left in the photo is 3½" Rolly Twiddle wearing her original outfit. Rolly was issued in 1967 and 1968. She came with either a pink, magenta, or orange wagon, and a pail and shovel also in pink, magenta, or orange. The color of her pail and shovel usually matched the color of her wagon's handle. 2" Lois Locket on the right in the photo was issued starting in 1967. The first issue of Lois came in a locket with a gold frame, yellow back, and green jewels like the one shown in the photo. In 1968 and 1969 Lois came in a locket with an orange back, green frame, and orange jewels. Both black Kiddles are difficult to find, especially mint and complete or NRFP/MOC. Rolly Twiddle/complete with all accessories: **$200.00 – 300.00.** Lois Locket doll and locket: **$75.00 – 125.00.**

Rolly Twiddle: A rare Rolly Twiddle mint-on-small-card with magenta colored pail and shovel. MOSC: **$400.00 – 600.00.** *Courtesy Robin Englehart, vintagelane.com, photo by Nancy Jean Mong.*

Sleeping Biddle: Sleeping Biddle came with three variations of headwear: a satin ribbon hair bow with a rhinestone in the center (most common), a round gold bead tiara, or a three-strand hair band of pearls like on the doll in the photo. 3½" Sleeping Biddle is shown sleeping on her claw-foot chaise lounge. The doll's outfit includes her dress, an often missing purple belt, pink pantaloons, and hard-to-find pink bow shoes. Doll completely dressed with chaise lounge: **$95.00 – 130.00.**

Sleeping Biddle: Mattel put out a series of Storybook Kiddles including Alice in Wonderliddle, Cinderiddle, Liddle Biddle Peep, Liddle Middle Muffet, Liddle Red Riding Hiddle, Peter Paniddle, and Sleeping Biddle. Alice in Wonderliddle, Cinderiddle, and Sleeping Biddle were sold not only individually but also inside a carrying case/playhouse. Here is Sleeping Biddle with her play castle. Complete set with castle: **$200.00 – 250.00.**

Tracy Trikediddle Pedal Party Set: Skediddle Kiddles dolls were a set of Liddle Kiddles who could walk with the help of a Skediddler walker that snapped into a button on the Skediddle Kiddles' backs. Some Kiddles came with just a Skediddler walker, while others came in Ride 'N Run sets with both a walker and a pedal toy. Here is a rare Skediddle Kiddle Pedal Party Set. The set features a Tracy Trikediddle with a helicopter, tricycle with wagon, and Skediddler/walker. Most Tracy Trikediddle dolls came in a set with just a tricycle with a wagon and a Skediddler. Mint/complete set with box: **$250.00 – 350.00.** *Courtesy Robin Englehart, vintagelane.com, photo by Nancy Jean Mong.*

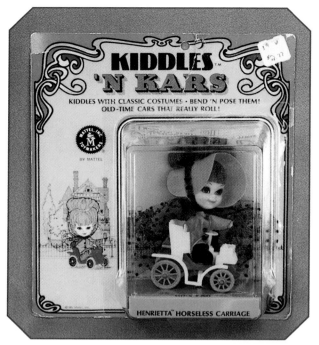

Kiddles 'N Cars: Kiddles 'N Cars were a set of 2⅞" Kiddle dolls dressed in classic antique costumes that came riding in plastic antique style cars. The four Kiddles 'N Cars dolls included Henrietta Horseless Carriage, Lenore Limousine, Rosemary Roadster, and Teresa Touring Car. Shown in the photo is Henrietta Horseless Carriage in her original package. NRFP: **$150.00 – 200.00.**

Lucky Locket Kiddles: Back of Laverne's box showing the six reissued Lucky Locket Kiddles. *Courtesy Robin Englehart, vintagelane.com, photo by Nancy Jean Mong.*

Lucky Locket Kiddles: Lucky Locket Kiddles were 2" tall Liddle Kiddles dolls packaged inside plastic lockets. Each locket had a chain so it could be worn as a necklace or it could be displayed like a picture frame by pulling out a stand built into the back of the locket. The doll inside could be taken out of the locket for play. All together there were 14 different Lucky Locket Kiddles. In 1975 after Liddle Kiddles had been off the shelves for some time, Mattel reissued six of the original Locket Kiddles. The dolls were a harder vinyl than the earlier dolls and came with painted on panties rather than the cloth panties the earlier dolls had. The lockets were sold on a cardboard backing like the original Locket Kiddles. The difference was the card was now placed inside a box with a plastic window front. The box was dated 1978 and the card was dated 1976. The reissued Locket Kiddle shown here is Laverne. Mint/complete set with box: **$55.00 – 85.00.** *Courtesy Robin Englehart, vintagelane.com, photo by Nancy Jean Mong.*

152

Kola Kiddles: 2" Liddle Kiddle dolls called Kola Kiddles came packaged inside plastic soda pop bottles. The six different Kola Kiddles included Laffy Lemon, Greta Grape, Kleo Kola, Luscious Lime, Oliva Orange, and Shirley Strawberry. Shown in the photo is Olivia Orange still on her original card. NRFC: **$100.00 – 125.00.**

Jewelry Kiddles: The tiny Jewelry Kiddle dolls are approximately 1" in height. They were originally housed in plastic jewelry such as rings, bracelets, pins, or necklaces that could be opened up so the dolls could be taken out and played with. The jewelry was either in the shape of a heart or a flower. The doll on the left in the photo is just slightly under an inch tall and originally came inside the Liddle Kiddle heart pin. The doll on the right measures ¾" and originally came inside the heart ring. It was also sold with the Mini-Kiddles Popup Gingerbread House. Dolls without jewelry: **$10.00 – 25.00 each.**

Prototype Jewelry Kiddles: This photo shows a variety of prototype Jewelry Kiddle dolls and one Lucky Locket-sized doll which never made it into production. Not enough examples available to determine fair market value. *Courtesy Robin Englehart, vintagelane.com, photo by Nancy Jean Mong.*

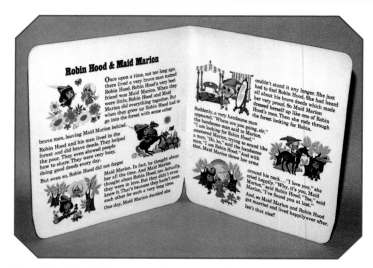

Storybook Kiddles Sweethearts: Robin Hood and Maid Marion's card opened to reveal their storybook. *Courtesy Robin Englehart, vintagelane.com, photo by Nancy Jean Mong.*

Storybook Kiddles Sweethearts: Four sets of Storybook Kiddles Sweethearts were put out by Mattel. The Kiddles came inside a card which opened up like a book to reveal a story about the Kiddles. The Storybook Kiddles came with a necklace with the dolls' portraits molded on it and two heart-shaped stands. Shown in the photo are Robin Hood and Maid Marion. Like all the Storybook Kiddles Sweethearts they are 2" tall. MOC: **$175.00 – 250.00.** *Courtesy Robin Englehart, vintagelane.com, photo by Nancy Jean Mong.*

Storybook Kiddles Sweethearts: Back of Robin Hood and Maid Marion's card showing the four different sets of Storybook Kiddles Sweethearts. *Courtesy Robin Englehart, vintagelane.com, photo by Nancy Jean Mong.*

Chitty Chitty Bang Bang Kiddles: The main characters from the movie *Chitty Chitty Bang Bang* were made into Kiddles. Mr. Potts and Truly Scrumptious were the only two Kiddles modeled after real people, Dick Van Dyke and Sally Ann Howes. The children, Jeremy and Jemima, although based on the characters in the movie bore little resemblance to the actors who played the parts, but instead looked more like the tiny Jewelry Liddle Kiddles dolls. Mr. Potts and Truly Scruptious Kiddles were 2" tall. Jeremy and Jemima Kiddles were ⅞" tall. Loose Mr. Potts or Truly Scrumptious with stands: **$35.00 – 45.00 each.** Jeremy or Jemima loose with stands: **$20.00 – 25.00 each.** Set of four dolls with stands: **$95.00 – 150.00.**

Peanuts/Disney/Warner Brothers Skediddlers: Technically these dolls aren't Liddle Kiddles, but because they use the Skediddle Kiddles body and/or arms, they are often lumped in the category of Liddle Kiddles. Like the Skediddle Kiddles, these characters walk with the help of a Skediddler walker that snapped into a button on the dolls' backs. Markings on the dolls are as follows:

Bugs Bunny
Head: "©1969 Mattel, Inc./Hong Kong/© Warner Bros. 7 Arts Inc."
Body: "U.S. & Foreign Pat Pend /©1969 Mattel Inc./©Warner Bros. 7 Arts"
Donald Duck, Mickey Mouse, Goofy
Head: "©Walt Disney Productions/©1968 Mattel Inc. Hong Kong"
Body: "©1968/Mattel, Inc./Mexico/U.S. Pat. Pend."
Lucy
Head: "©1952 United Features/©1968 Mattel, Inc./Hong Kong"
Body: "©1967/Mattel Inc./Mexico/U.S. Pat. Pend."
Charlie Brown
Head: "©1968 Mattel Inc./Hong Kong/©1950 United Features"
Body: "©1967/Mattel Inc./Mexico/U.S. Pat. Pend"
Snoopy
Head: "©1950 United Features/©1968 Mattel, Inc./Hong Kong"
Body: "©1968/Mattel, Inc./Mexico / U.S. Pat. Pend."
 Skediddlers mint and complete: **$30.00 – 45.00**. *Courtesy Mark A. Salyers.*

Linus Skediddler: Linus is the hardest member of the Skediddler Peanuts gang to find. When loose, he usually is missing his cloth blanket. NRFB: **$275.00 – 350.00**. *Courtesy Michele Casino.*

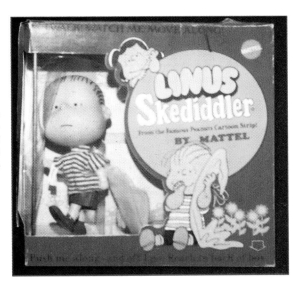

Sweet Treats: In 1979 after Kiddles had been discontinued, Mattel came out with another small set of dolls called Sweet Treats. The Sweet Treat dolls came packaged inside plastic ice cream sundaes, ice cream bars, cookies, or spoons. Many collectors think of Sweet Treats as being part of the Kiddle line since they are very similar in appearance to Kiddles. The biggest difference is that Sweet Treat dolls were jointed at the thighs rather than having a wire through their bendable legs. A lot of old stock of Sweet Treats has been floating around the collectibles market for a number of years, so finding them still in their original box is fairly easy. The NRFB gift set in the photo, however, is uncommon. NRFB: **$45.00 – 75.00.** *Courtesy Robin Englehart, vintagelane.com, photo by Nancy Jean Mong.*

Sweet Treats: Back of the Sweet Treats gift set box. *Courtesy Robin Englehart, vintagelane.com, photo by Nancy Jean Mong.*

Upsy Downsy: Upsy Downsys are small dolls that are colorful, fun, and a little bit on the bizarre side. According to the storybook Welcome to Upsy Downsy Land, the Upsy Downsys started life as dandelions. A blustery wind blew into town, but the dandelions tickled the wind's nose so he blew them all away. When the dandelions fell back to earth the next morning, some of them drifted through a rainbow and changed into funny little people. They landed right side-up so they were called Upsys. Others fell into a storm cloud and came out looking like silly people. When they fell to earth they landed on the ground on their heads and hands so they were called Downsys. The Upsy are 2½" tall and the Downsys are 3½". They are marked "©1969 MATTEL, INC./HONG KONG" on their heads. Upsy Downsy dolls came with a vehicle and several small accessories as well as a playland board that could connect to all the other Upsy Downsy playland boards. There were also story books featuring the dolls. The Upsys included Baby So High, Flossy Glossy, Foozie Woozie, Furry Hurry Wiz-z-zer, Hithery Thithery, Pudgy Fudgy, Tickle Pinkle, and Tingle Dingle. The Downsys included Downy Dilly, Gooey Chooey, Miss Information, Mother What Now, Pocus Hocus, Skelter Helter, and Short Order.

Upsys: From left to right are Baby So-High and her Airo-Zoomer, Flossy Glossy and her Elewetter Fire-Truck, Tickle Pinkle with her Bugabout and mushroom gas pump, and Pudgy Fudgy and her Piggybus. Loose pieces: **$10.00 – 30.00 each.** *Courtesy Karen Hickey.*

Downsys: From left to right are Miss Information (missing glasses) and her Booth Moose, Pocus Hocus and his Dragon Wagon, Mother What Now and her Go-Getter, and Downy Dilly and her Footmobile. Loose pieces: **$10.00 – 30.00 each.** *Courtesy Karen Hickey.*

Upsy Downsy: The Upsy Downsy playsets in the photos are The Happy Go Round and included Upsy dolls Tingle Dingle and Foozie Woozie. Complete in original box set: **$95.00 – 175.00.**
Courtesy Robin Englehart, vintagelane.com, photo by Nancy Jean Mong.

Bouncy Baby: 10½" Bouncy Baby's head and limbs were attached with elastic cords that allowed the doll to bounce and move freely. She was available in 1969. Bouncy Baby is basically the same doll as Baby Go Bye-Bye, which was available in 1970 wearing different clothing and sporting a different hairstyle. The 1971 Montgomery Wards catalog actually showed a Bouncy Baby in Baby Go Bye-Bye's buggy and advertised her as being Baby Go Bye-Bye, even though their catalog the year before featured the correct Baby Go Bye-Bye in her buggy. It may be possible that left-over stock of Bouncy Baby dolls was used with left-over Baby Go Bye-Bye's buggies and sold together under the name Baby Go Bye-Bye, but so far the author hasn't seen any NRFB sets that would confirm that. J.C. Penneys and Sears did not show either Bouncy Baby or Baby Go Bye-Bye in their Christmas catalogs that year so it's possible only Wards was selling leftover pieces from both dolls. Bouncy Baby is marked "©1968 MATTEL, INC./HONG KONG" on her head and "©1968 MATTEL, INC./MEXICO/U.S. PATENT PENDING" on her lower back. In the photo she is shown still attached to her original cardboard insert from her box. Mint on original card: **$75.00 – 95.00.**

Small Shots: 5" Small Shots came with roller skates hooked on their feet to race down tracks. Shown in the photo are Funny Fran and Nifty Nan in their original packages. NRFP: **$75.00 – 125.00.**
Courtesy Michele Casino.

Sketchy: 19" Sketchy comes with a drawing table and 12 embossed templates. She draws or writes her name by moving a magnetic crayon holder across her drawing table top, bringing out the highlights of the templates. Sketchy is marked "©1969 Mattel, Inc. /U.S. Patent Pending /USA" on her back. Mint with box and desk: **$75.00 – 95.00.** *Courtesy Mark A. Salyers.*

Small Shots: Funny Fran and Nifty Nan shown out of their packages. Loose: **$25.00 – 45.00.** *Courtesy Michele Casino.*

Small Shot Skate and Race Set: The Small Shots dolls could be used with Mattel's Hot Wheels tracks but this track set was made especially for them. The set came with two dolls, Sillie Millie and Red Hot Red. The set is hard to find. Track and dolls in original box: **$175.00 – 200.00.** *Courtesy Michele Casino.*

Small Shots: 5" Sillie Millie and Red Hot Red, the two Small Shots dolls that came inside the Skate and Race set. Loose dolls: **$35.00 – 45.00 each.** *Courtesy Michele Casino.*

Small Shots: Three Mattel Small Shots dolls Daredevil Dexter, Dartin' Darlene with her cart, and Breezy Bridgit. Loose: **$25.00 – 45.00.** *Courtesy Michele Casino.*

Super Small Shots: In 1972 the Small Shots line was expanded to include the Super Small Shots. Super Small Shots dolls came with a riding toy and had jointed waists. The photo shows the Super Small Shots Reckless Richard and his Go-Cart, Hasty Harriet and her Skate Crate, and Roarin' Rita and her Wagon. Super Small Shots dolls are hard to find. NRFP: **$125.00 – 350.00 each.** *Courtesy Michele Casino.*

Hi Dottie: 17" doll that came with two telephones; one doll-sized and the other child-sized. The receiver of the doll-sized phone plugs into Hi Dottie's left hand. When the receiver on the child-size phone is pressed Hi Dottie talks. She also talks if the button on her left wrist is pressed. Her box was meant to be cut so that it could be used as a phone booth for the doll. Hi Dottie is marked "©1969/MATTEL/INC./MEXICO" on her head and "©1971/MATTEL/INC./MEXICO/U.S. PATENT PEND." on her back. Doll with box and all accessories: **$55.00 – 85.00.** *Courtesy Mark A. Salyers.*

Baby Sing-A-Song: A 1969 – 1970 Sears exclusive doll. The 17½" pull-string doll sings songs and comes with a sing-along songbook. Baby Sing-A-Song is marked "©1969 MATTEL, INC./ MEXICO" on her head and "©1964 MATTEL, INC. /HAWTHORNE, CALIF., USA/PATENTED IN USA/PATENTED IN CANADA 1962/OTHER PATENTS PENDING/ MADE IN MEXICO" on her body. MIB/working: **$95.00 – 125.00.** *Courtesy Mark A. Salyers.*

161

Baby Flip-Flop: A 1970 – 1971 J.C. Penney exclusive 15" pull-string talker. The doll says four phrases when she is right side up or four different phrases when she is upside down standing on her head. Baby Flip-Flop is marked "©1968 MATTEL, INC./MEXICO" on her head and tagged "Quality Originals by Mattel®/Baby Flip Flop/©1969 Mattel, Inc./Hawthorne, Calif./Made in Mexico/ALL NEW MATERIALS/Consisting of: Polyurethane Foam.70%/ Shredded Clippings.30%/US Patented/Pat'd. in Canada 1969/Other Pats. Pend." on her cloth body. Talking: **$35.00 – 50.00.** *Courtesy Mark A. Salyers.*

Flossie: A Roarin' '20s Girl, this 11½" pull-string talking flapper speaks eight ragtime phrases. The other Roarin' '20s doll was Flo. Both Flossie and Flo were Sears exclusive dolls in 1969 and 1970. NRFB/talking: **$100.00 – 125.00.** *Courtesy Mark A. Salyers.*

Talk-A-Littles: Talk-A-Littles pull-string talking rag dolls included 6" Toofums, 7½" Roscoe, and 7" Sassie. Shown in the photo is Sassie. The doll is tagged "Quality Originals by/MATTEL® /TALK-A-LITTLES™/©1970 Mattel, Inc/Hawthorne, Calif./Made in Taiwan" along with material contents and other patent information. Talking: **$15.00 – 25.00.**

Cat in the Hat: 10" pull-string talking doll says things like "I like to be here," and "Does your mother know I'm here?" The doll has a plastic head and softed-stuffed body. The Cat in the Hat is tagged "Quality Originals by/MATTEL®/CAT IN THE HAT/©1970 DR. SEUSS/ALL RIGHTS RESERVED/Mattel, Inc/Hawthorne, Calif./Made in Hong Kong" along with material contents and other patent information. A larger pull-string talking Cat in the Hat was also produced by Mattel. Talking: **$35.00 – 50.00.**

Great Big Beautiful Bertha: Great Big Beautiful Bertha was a 40" stuffed doll with straps on her feet to attach around a child's feet so the child and the doll could dance together. The pull-string talking doll said ten different phrases. Originally in Bertha's pocket were eight colored pencils and a coloring book. In 1970 Montgomery Wards was the only major department store to show her in their Christmas catalog, but she was not advertised as being a Wards exclusive, so it is unknown if she was available in other stores as well. Her body is tagged "Quality Originals by Mattel®/©1969 Mattel, Inc. /Hawthorne, Calif./Made in Mexico/ALL NEW MATERIALS/Consisting of:/Pastel dyed Shredded Clippings. 40%/Polyurethane/Shredded Foam. 60% /U.S. & Foreign Patented/Pat'd. in Canada, 1962/Other Pats. Pending." Talking: **$50.00 – 75.00.** *Courtesy Mark A. Salyer.*

Best Friend Cynthia: 18½" Cynthia is a battery-operated talking doll that works with the help of a record inserted in a slot on her side. She uses the same head mold as Mattel's Quick Curl Casey doll. Cynthia has a vinyl head and limbs and a plastic torso. She is marked "©1971 MATTEL INC./HONG/KONG" on her head and "©1971 MATTEL, INC./U.S.A./U.S. PATENT PENDING" on the record button on her back. Re-dressed and not working: **$10.00 – 15.00.** MIB/working: **$50.00 – 65.00.**
Courtesy Robin Englehart, vintagelane.com, photo by Nancy Jean Mong.

Rock Flowers: 6½" dolls representing hip rock stars. Each doll originally came with a record that had holes in the center to place a plastic stand in. The doll could then be placed in the stand and would spin around and dance to the music when it was played on a record player. Rock Flowers dolls have poseable limbs due to a wire inside their vinyl bodies. The original Rock Flowers dolls included blond hair Heather, Lilac with red hair, and African-American doll Rosemary. Later Iris and Doug joined the group. Mattel sold a variety of fashions separately for the Rock Flowers, and today it isn't too difficult to locate many of these fashions still in their original package. Rock Flowers dolls are marked "©MATTEL INC./1970 HONG KONG" on their heads and "HONG KONG/1970 MATTEL, INC./U.S. & FOR. PAT'D/PAT'D IN CANADA" on their backs. From left to right in photo: Rosemary wearing her original outfit, Lilac wearing Iris's original outfit, Heather wearing her original outfit, Doug wearing his original outfit, and Lilac wearing her original outfit. Missing from photo is Iris. **$15.00 – 20.00 each.** *Courtesy Robin Englehart, vintagelane.com, photo by Nancy Jean Mong.*

Rock Flowers Rosemary: Rosemary shown in her original box. MIB **$40.00 – 55.00.** *Courtesy Robin Englehart, vintagelane.com, photo by Nancy Jean Mong.*

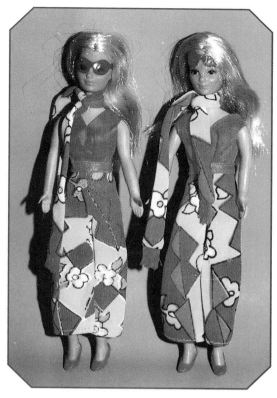

Rock Flowers Heather: Two Heather dolls in their original outfits. **$15.00 – 20.00 each.** *Courtesy Robin Englehart, vintagelane.com, photo by Nancy Jean Mong.*

Rock Flowers Rosemary: Rosemary shown wearing fashion #4051 Skirted in Fringe, a Rock Flowers outfit sold separately. Doll with outfit: **$15.00 – 20.00.** *Courtesy Robin Englehart, vintagelane.com, photo by Nancy Jean Mong.*

Rock Flowers Rosemary: Rosemary shown wearing Rock Flowers outfit #4052 Jeans in Fringe. Doll with outfit: **$15.00 – 20.00.** *Courtesy Robin Englehart, vintagelane.com, photo by Nancy Jean Mong.*

Rock Flowers Heather: Heather wearing Rock Flowers fashion #4053 Tie Dye Maxi. Doll with outfit: **$15.00 – 20.00.** *Courtesy Robin Englehart, vintagelane.com, photo by Nancy Jean Mong.*

Rock Flowers Heather: Heather shown wearing fashion #4056 Mini Lace. Doll with outfit: **$15.00 – 20.00.** *Courtesy Robin Englehart, vintagelane.com, photo by Nancy Jean Mong.*

Rock Flowers Heather: Heather wearing Rock Flowers fashion #4057 Flares 'n Lace. Doll with outfit: **$15.00 – 20.00.** *Courtesy Robin Englehart, vintagelane.com, photo by Nancy Jean Mong.*

Rock Flowers Lilac: Lilac wearing Rock Flowers outfit #4058 Topped in Lace. Doll with outfit: **$15.00 – 20.00.** *Courtesy Robin Englehart, vintagelane.com, photo by Nancy Jean Mong.*

Rock Flowers Lilac: Lilac shown wearing #4066 Overall Blue. Doll with outfit: **$15.00 – 20.00.** *Courtesy Robin Englehart, vintagelane.com, photo by Nancy Jean Mong.*

Rock Flowers Lilac: Lilac wearing Rock Flowers outfit #4069 Frontier Gingham. Doll with outfit: **$15.00 – 20.00.** *Courtesy Robin Englehart, vintagelane.com, photo by Nancy Jean Mong.*

Rock Flowers Fashion: Rock Flowers fashion #4070 Frontier Flowers in its original package. NRFP: **$20.00 – 25.00.** *Courtesy Robin Englehart, vintagelane.com, photo by Nancy Jean Mong.*

Rock Flowers Iris: Iris wearing Rock Flowers fashion #4071 Indian Poncho. Doll with outfit: **$15.00 – 20.00.** *Courtesy Robin Englehart, vintagelane.com, photo by Nancy Jean Mong.*

Rock Flowers Lilac: Lilac shown wearing fashion #4072 Indian Midi. Doll with outfit: **$15.00 – 20.00.** *Courtesy Robin Englehart, vintagelane.com, photo by Nancy Jean Mong.*

Rock Flowers Iris: Iris shown wearing #4073 Indian Gaucho. Doll with outfit: **$15.00 – 20.00.** *Courtesy Robin Englehart, vintagelane.com, photo by Nancy Jean Mong.*

167

Rock Flowers Case: The Rock Flowers On Stage Case is a carrying case that doubles as a stage/play structure to use with the Rock Flowers dolls. The case originally came with two speakers and a floor length microphone. Inside there are three compartments for the dolls, a place to store three records, and a small compartment for clothing and accessories. Case with accessories: **$25.00 – 35.00.** Case without accessories: **$15.00 – 20.00.** *Courtesy Robin Englehart, vintagelane.com, photo by Nancy Jean Mong.*

Timey Tell: Timey Tell had a "magic" watch that when her talking ring was pulled she would tell you the time and say a different phrase for each hour. The doll came with many accessories and a child-size watch which matched the watch on Timey's wrist. 16" Timey Tell is marked "©1969 MATTEL, INC. MEXICO" on her head and "©1964 MATTEL, INC./HAWTHORNE, CALIFORNIA U.S.A./PATENTED IN U.S.A. PATENTED/IN CANADA 1962 OTHER/PATENTS PENDING MADE IN MEXICO" on her back. MIB/talking: **$55.00 – 85.00.** *Courtesy Mark A. Salyers.*

Shoppin' Sheryl: Shoppin' Sheryl is 14½" with a vinyl head and a plastic body and limbs. A magnet inside her right palm and a moveable thumb on her left hand allow Sheryl to hold items. Two buttons on her sides work the moveable thumb. She came with a shopping cart, groceries, paper grocery bags, play money, and display shelves with her name on them. Sheryl is marked "©1970 MATTEL, INC. HONG KONG" on her head and "©1970 MATTEL, INC./MEXICO/U.S. PATENT PENDING"" on her back. MIB: **$55.00 – 85.00.** *Courtesy Mark A. Salyers.*

Busy Becky: A Busy Becky doll was offered in either a housekeeping set or in a Surprise Garden set. In addition to the housekeeping set with the doll, the housekeeping accessories could be purchased separately without a doll. In 1972 Montgomery Wards offered an exclusive Busy Becky and her Surprise Garden set. The doll in the photograph is shown with the original box and accessories from the housekeeping set, as well as the accessories from the gardening set. The same doll was included in both sets. Becky is holding the unpunched gardening tools, and the yellow trellises for the flowerpots are in front of the Housekeeping box. Her original box for the gardening set was a brown shipping box with "Caution: Live Plants" on the top. Busy Becky is marked "©1970 Mattel, Inc./Hong Kong" on her head and "©1970 Mattel, Inc./Mexico/U.S. Patent Pending" on her body. MIB with housekeeping accessories: **$65.00 – 85.00.** *Courtesy Mark A. Salyers.*

Talking Mother Goose: A 20" pull-string talking doll with a vinyl head and a stuffed body and limbs. Talking Mother Goose is fairly easy to locate and demand for her has been relatively low so she can still be found at reasonable prices. Working: **$20.00 – 25.00.**
Courtesy Robin Englehart, vintagelane.com, photos by Nancy Jean Mong.

Baby Play-a-Lot: Baby Play-a-Lot from 1972 plays with her toys when you press a switch and pull her string. 15" Baby Play-a-Lot is marked "©1971 Mattel, Inc./Hong Kong" on her head and "©1971 Mattel, Inc./Hong Kong/U.S. Patent Pending" on her body. MIB/working: **$45.00 – 75.00.** *Courtesy Mark A. Salyers.*

Big Jim: With anti-war sentiment running high in the early-1970s, Mattel decided to come out with an action figure for boys that was less geared towards military play and instead geared more towards sports and outdoorsmen adventures. Mattel's 9" Big Jim and his friends had well articulated bodies with biceps that actually flexed and a special action movement in the arms that when a button was pressed on the back of the figure, the right arm would go down. Mattel's Big Jim action figures were produced for the U.S. market from 1973 through 1976, but continued to be sold for the European market into the mid-1980s. There were two series of the Big Jim collection. The first series was the all-Star series. The figures in the All-Star series included Big Jim, Big Josh, Big Jack, Big Jeff, and Dr. Steel. The P.A.C.K. series for Big Jim was issued in 1976. P.A.C.K. stood for Professional Agents Crime Killers. Now Big Jim and his pals were geared more for spy adventures and fighting crime than sports and outdoorsmen adventures. The figures in the P.A.C.K. series included Big Jim, The Whip, Warpath, Dr. Steel, Torpedo Fist, and Zorak. This page from Montgomery Wards 1973 Christmas Catalog shows some of the figures and accessories in the Big Jim line that year. MIB Big Jim dolls: **$60.00 – 180.00** depending on rarity. NRFP outfits: **$25.00 – 75.00** depending on rarity.

1 Sky Commander **10**⁸⁷ Over 4 ft. long!

Folds into 14 in. high carry case

2 **9**⁷⁷

Kung Fu Studio

with exercise gear and kickout wall. Muscle Mover lets all Big Jim® figures move realistically!

12 in. high carry case

Big Jim® Jungle Adventures—
Authentic gear, plus animals, too

3

4

5

6 Big Jack®
7 Big Jim®
8 Big Josh
9 Big Jeff

STAND BY FOR INSTRUCTIONS

10 Talking Big Jim

392 JCPenney

2⁷⁷ Each—Any 2 for **5**⁰⁰

11 12 13 14

Big Jim: This catalog shows some of the accessories available for Big Jim. *J.C. Penney 1974 Christmas Catalog.*

Sunshine Family: The Sunshine extended family included a 9½" grandfather and a 9" grandmother. The grandparents came in a set of two dolls. Both Grandpa and Grandma Sunshine are marked "©1975/ TAIWAN/ MATTEL, INC." on their heads and "©1973/ MATTEL, INC./TAIWAN" on their backs. NRFB: **$45.00 – 65.00 each.**

Sunshine Family: In 1974 Mattel introduced the Sunshine Family, consisting of the father Steve, the mother Steffie, and baby Sweets. The three dolls were sold as a set. Steve is 9½", Steffie is 9", and Sweets is 3". All three dolls are marked "©1973/MATTEL, INC." on their heads and "©1973/MATTEL, INC./TAIWAN" on their backs. In 1978, the last year the Sunshine Family appeared in major department store catalogs, a sister was added to the line. The 4¾" sister came in a set with the other three family members and is not as common as the others since she wasn't available as long. It is believed the sister was Baby Sweets grown older and that a new baby boy was added to the family. Little Sister is marked "©1977/MATTEL, INC. /TAIWAN" on her head and "©Mattel, Inc. 1977/TAIWAN," on her back. Steffie/Steve: $15.00 – 20.00 each. Sweets: **$10.00 – 12.00.** Little Sister: **$20.00 – 25.00.** *Courtesy Robin Englehart, vintagelane.com, photo by Nancy Jean Mong.*

Happy Family: The black friends of the Sunshine family included a 9½" father Hal, a 9" mother Hattie, and their 3" baby Hon. Like the other Sunshine Family, the Happy Family was only available as a set. NRFB: **$55.00 – 75.00 each.**

Love Notes Doll: 13" Melody Love Notes. The doll is missing her original head scarf. **$10.00 – 15.00.** *Courtesy Robin Englehart, vintagelane.com, photo by Nancy Jean Mong.*

Love Notes Doll: In 1975 Mattel introduced their line of Love Notes dolls. When the doll's hands, feet, or stomach was pressed, a different musical note was played. By following a color-coded songbook that was included with the dolls and by pressing the corresponding colored notes on the dolls' bodies, children could play songs such as *Jingle Bells, Three Blind Mice, Row, Row, Row Your Boat, The Farmer in the Dell, Home on the Range,* and *Mary Had a Little Lamb.* The 13" Love Notes dolls included Nellie (auburn hair), Bucky (cowboy), Melody (blond hair), and Lilty (African-American). Shown in photo is Nellie. NRFB: **$35.00 – 40.00.** Loose: **$10.00 – 15.00.**

L'il Love Notes Doll: Starting in 1979 smaller Love Notes dolls were also made. These dolls were 10" and included Swingy and Kelly. The dolls are marked "©MATTEL INC. 1974/TAI-WAN" on their necks and tagged "©MATTEL, INC. 1974/Hawthorn, Ca. 90250/MADE IN TAI-WAN/ALL NEW MATERIALS" on their bodies along with material content and regulation number. The L'il Love Notes Dolls were not sold as long as the 13" dolls and so consequently are a little harder to find. Shown in the photo is 10" L'il Love Notes Swingy next to 13" Love Notes Nellie. Loose Swingy: **$10.00 – 15.00.**

Rosebud: Mattel's 4½" Rosebud dolls were named after miniature roses. The dolls included A Baby Darling Rose, A Baby Gold Star Rose, A Scarlet Gem Rose, A Lavender Lace Rose, A Baby White Star Rose, and A Pink Heather Rose. The doll in the photo is Scarlet Gem. Her box is dated 1976. MIB: **$15.00 – 20.00.**

Rosebud: Mattel also made Rosebud dolls in a 7" size. Shown in the photo is Silvie. The other two 7" Rosebud dolls included Stella (black doll) and Marissa (red hair). MIB: **$20.00 – 35.00.** *Courtesy Kathleen Tornikoski, Romancing the Doll.*

Rosebud: Some Rosebud dolls came with baby accessories. This 4½" Darling Rose doll was sold with a cradle. The doll is marked "©MATTEL INC./1976/TAIWAN" on her head and back. Loose doll with cradle: **$10.00 – 15.00.**

Marie Osmond: A Marie Osmond doll shown in her original box. NRFB: **$35.00 – 45.00 each.** *Courtesy Robin Englehart, vintagelane.com, photo by Nancy Jean Mong.*

Donny and Marie Osmond: These dolls were issued in 1976 when *The Donny and Marie Show* was airing on television. Marie is an 11½" Barbie-size doll. She is marked "©MATTEL, INC. /1966/KOREA" on her lower body. Donny is 11¾" and marked "1088 0500 2/©MATTEL/INC. 1968 HONG KONG" on his back. These dolls are common and easily found. **$15.00 – 25.00 each.** *Courtesy Robin Englehart, vintagelane.com, photo by Nancy Jean Mong.*

Welcome Back, Kotter: The main characters from the television show, *Welcome Back, Kotter,* were made into dolls in 1976. The five dolls were available in this deluxe classroom set, but the 9" dolls were also sold individually as well. Their bodies and jointed limbs were similar to Mattel's Sunshine Family line of dolls. Set of five dolls with classroom set: **$100.00 – 175.00.** *Courtesy Sharon Criscione.*

Kate Jackson, Cheryl Ladd, Kitty O'Neil: Celebrity dolls in their original boxes, circa 1978. MIB: **$75.00 each.** *Courtesy Hillary and Cliff James, Toy with Me.*

Gorgeous Creatures: 7½", these unusual fashion dolls had shapely female figures but the heads of animals. Mattel's Gorgeous Creatures included Cow Belle at the Beauty Shop, Ms. Giddee Yup at the Dress Shop, Ms. Heavenly Hippo at the China Shop, and Princess Pig at the Restaurant. The dolls weren't too popular with children and today are often found still in their original boxes. Shown in the photo is Princess Pig. MIB: **$20.00 – 25.00.**

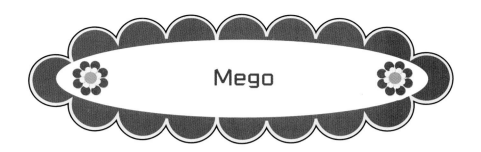

Mego

Broadway Joe Namath and His Mod-About Town Wardrobe: A 12" doll made in the image of football-quarterback-turned-actor Joe Namath came out in 1970. Some of his outfits which were sold separately included Bachelor, Eligible Receiver, In Vest, Furward Pass, Different Drummer, and more. All the outfits were very mod looking. Because the 12" figure was more like a fashion doll than an action figure, it held little appeal to either boys or girls at the time. Joe is shown in the photo wearing his original football uniform along with his NRFB Tuff Tux outfit. Loose doll: **$30.00 – 50.00.** NRFB outfit: **$25.00 – 45.00.** *Courtesy Hillary and Cliff James, Toy with Me.*

Joe Namath: Close-up of Mego's Joe Namath doll. *Courtesy Hillary and Cliff James, Toy with Me.*

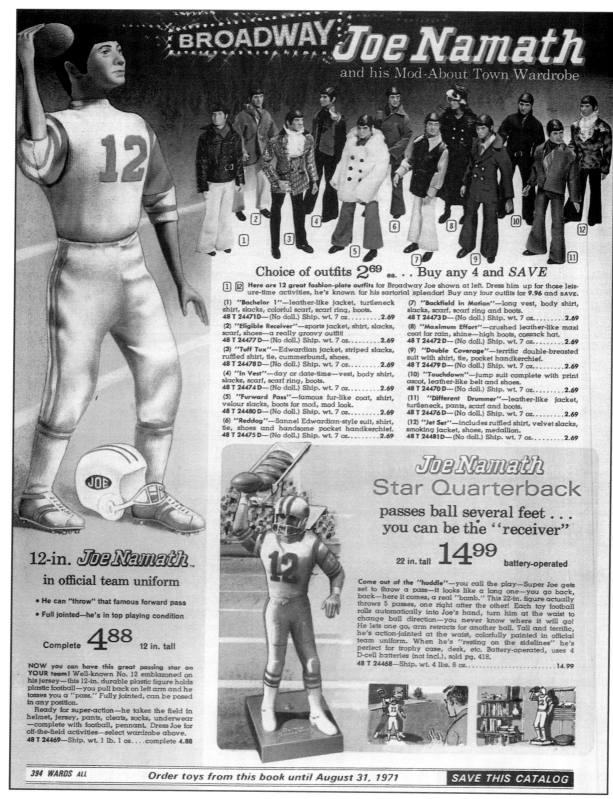

Joe Namath: Montgomery Wards 1970 Christmas catalog showing Joe Namath and his wardrobe.

Wizard of Oz: 8" dolls, Dorothy, Tin Woodsman, Scarecrow, and Cowardly Lion. NRFB: **$25.00 – 45.00 each.** *Courtesy Michele Casino.*

Wizard of Oz: 8" dolls, The Wicked Witch and Glinda the Good Witch. Wicked Witch, NRFB: **$35.00 – 65.00.** Glinda, NRFB: **$25.00 – 45.00.** *Courtesy Michele Casino.*

Suzanne Somers: Doll made in the image of Suzanne Somers in the role of Chrissy from the television sitcom *Three's Company*. The 12¼" doll is shown with her original box. Doll with original box (missing shoes): **$35.00 – 55.00.**

Suzanne Somers: The 12¼" Suzanne Somers/Chrissy doll is shown with the back of her box. Mint with box: **$45.00 – 75.00.** *Courtesy Michele Casino.*

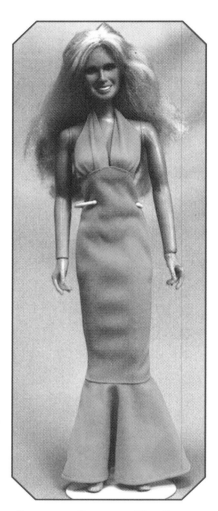

Suzanne Somers: The Suzanne Somers doll is marked "©Three's Company" on her neck and, "©MEGO CORP. 1975/MADE IN HONG KONG" on her back. **$20.00 – 30.00.**

Dinah-mite: 8" fully poseable fashion doll. Here she is shown in an unusual metallic jumpsuit. Numerous fashions were available separately for Dinah-mite. MIB: **$30.00 – 45.00.** *Courtesy Kathleen Tornikoski, Romancing the Doll.*

Dinah-mite: Dinah-mite shown in her original purple outfit and the jumpsuit from fashion #1402 Racing Around which was sold separately. **$20.00 – 25.00 each.** *Courtesy Robin Englehart, vintagelane.com, photo by Nancy Jean Mong.*

Dinah-mite: This Dinah-mite outfit is fashion #1410 Roller Derby. MIB outfit: **$25.00 – 35.00.** *Courtesy Robin Englehart, vintagelane.com, photo by Nancy Jean Mong.*

Dinah-mite: This is fashion #1403 Up, Up and Away. It also came in olive green. MIB outfit: **$25.00 – 35.00.** *Courtesy Robin Englehart, vintagelane.com, photo by Nancy Jean Mong.*

Kristy McNichol: Doll representing television actress Kristy McNichol. The 9½" doll is marked "©MEGO CORP./ MADE IN HONG KONG" on her head and "©1977 MEGO CORP./MADE IN HONG KONG" on her back. The year before another doll of McNichol was manufactured by Mattel, only it was marketed as Kristy McNichol as Buddy, the character McNichol played on the television show *Family*. MIB: **$35.00 – 45.00.** *Courtesy Michele Casino.*

World's Greatest Super Heroes: Mego produced many different 8" super heroes starting in 1972 and continuing through the late 1970s. The figures were sold in a variety of different window boxes or on cardboard backings with a bubble window like those in the photo. Depending on which issue the doll is, the value can vary. Shown in the photo are Spiderman, Superman, and Captain America. Spiderman, MOC, orange card: **$90.00 – 140.00.** Superman, MOC, yellow card: **$90.00 – 140.00.** Captain America, MOC, red card: **$150.00 – 250.00.** *Courtesy Robin Englehart, vintagelane.com, photo by Nancy Jean Mong.*

World's Greatest Super Heroes: Back of packages of figures showing some of the action figure characters available from Mego. *Courtesy Robin Englehart, vintagelane.com, photo by Nancy Jean Mong.*

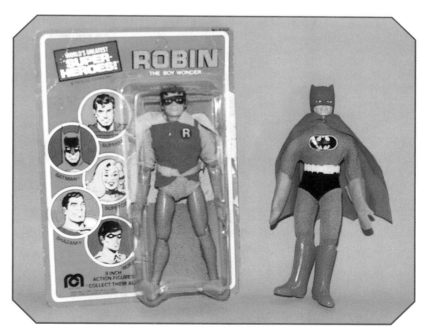

World's Greatest Super Heroes: 8" action figures of Robin and Batman. Robin, MOC, blue card: **$75.00 – 135.00.** Loose and complete Batman: **$50.00 – 90.00 each.** *Courtesy Robin Englehart, vintagelane.com, photo by Nancy Jean Mong.*

Batman and Robin Fight Their Archenemies

You create their exciting escapades!

[1] **Batcave© Playset With Signal*.** Secret entrance for batmobile, landing platform for 'copter, garage for cycle. Flash Batsignal to warn Dynamic Duo of danger—uses 2 "C" cell batteries (not incl.—order below). Batpole and "computer" included. Vinyl-covered cardboard, 43x15½x11¼ in. high. Action figures shown not included. Mailable.
X 923-0962 A—Wt. 3.50 lbs........13.66

"C"-Cell Batteries. Package of 6.
X 959-0787 A—Mail. wt. 0.95 lb.....1.29

[2] to [5] **Fist Fighting Action Figures.*** Button-operated to punch it out in the battle of good against evil—or adjust the arms easily and POW, they're karate fighters, with realistic karate blows! 8-in. plastic figures with vinyl heads. Each jointed figure is fully and authentically costumed.* Mail. wt. 0.40 lb. ea.
X 924-2363 A—[2] Robin©.........4.44
X 924-2488 A—[3] Riddler©.......4.44
X 924-2389 A—[4] Joker©.........4.44
X 924-2348 A—[5] Batman©.......4.44
SAVE 38c when you buy any two of [2] to [5] together. *State both Catalog Numbers and pay only.* 8.50
©*National Periodicals Publication, Inc.*

[6] **Super Hero™ Carrying Case.** Holds four 8-in. figures. Vinyl-covered cardboard, plastic handle. 12½x2¼x9½ in. high. Mailable.
X 923-1010 A—Wt. 1.20 lbs.........2.99

Comic Book Characters

[7] & [8] **Poseable 8-In. Action Figures*** of comic book heroes. Plastic with vinyl heads. Detailed, accurate costumes. Mail. wt. 0.40 lb.
X 924-2520 A—[7] The Hulk©......2.74
X 924-2512 A—[8] The Falcon©....2.74
SAVE 48c when you buy [7] & [8] together. *State both Catalog Numbers and pay only.*..........................5.00
© *1974 Marvel Comics Group*

[9] to [11] **Poseable 8-In. Female Action Figures.*** Dressed for action. Plastic and vinyl construction. Mail. wt. 0.40 lb. ea.
[9] **Wonder Woman©.**
X 923-0756 A.....................3.74
X 923-0897 A—[10] Bat Girl©.....3.74
X 923-0913 A—[11] Catwoman©..3.74
SAVE 48c when you buy any two of [9] to [11] together. *State both Catalog Numbers, pay only*..............7.00

[12] & [13] **Mobile Vans.*** Dynamic Duo and Joker can fight it out in the streets of Gotham City from within their mobile vans. Both have revolving platform for observation through the roof. Polystyrene 15½x7¾x8¾ in. vans fit any 8-in. figure. Figures shown not included.
[12] **Mobile Bat Lab©.** Includes batwinch with grappling hook, bat rope, and cage trap.
X 924-2579 A—Mail. wt. 4.50 lbs...12.66
[13] **Jokermobile©.** With laugh machine, front-end squirt flower, and rear boxing glove trap.
X 924-2611 A—Mail. wt. 4.50 lbs...12.66
© *National Periodicals Publications, 1973*

[14] & [15] **Authentic Bat Vehicles©.*** Plastic. Fit any 8-in. figures. Figures shown not included.
[14] **Batcycle** with side car for Robin. 10 in. long.
X 923-0731 A—Mail.: wt. 1 lb......5.99
[15] **Batmobile.** 13 in. long.
X 923-0749 A—Mail.: wt. 1 lb...... 5.99

Caution: toy with small parts—see note on page 392.

Batcave Playset 13⁶⁶

Button-Operated Super Heroes™ Slug It Out Against Super Foes™ 4⁴⁴ each figure any two for **8⁵⁰**

BAM! OOF! POW!

[6] 2.99

The Hulk **The Falcon** 2⁷⁴ each or 2 for 5⁰⁰

BatGirl Catwoman 3⁷⁴ or any 2 for 7⁰⁰ Wonder Woman

[12] to [15] Vehicles for On-the-Move Super Heroes **Mobile Vans 12⁶⁶ each**

Bat Vehicles 5⁹⁹ each

JCPenney 403

World's Greatest Super Heroes: J.C. Penneys 1975 Christmas catalog showing some of the Mego Super Heroes and their accessories available that year.

184

Exclusive at Wards!
3⁶⁹

A Direct from your favorite Saturday morning TV show—Isis, the mysterious maiden with magical powers to bring you exciting adventures. Bendable poseable 8-inch tall figure in special costume with "magic" medallion. Only at Wards!
48 G 24561—Ship. wt. 5 oz. 3.69

B Jokermobile. Joker zooms about in 14-in. long van made of high-impact polystyrene. Includes: flower that squirts water, trap that releases boxing glove, revolving platform inside. Figure not incl.
48 G 24727—Ship. wt. 4 lbs. 8 oz. 14.99

C Shiny and sleek, the 13-in. Batmobile is scaled to carry the dynamic duo on their escapades. Made of sturdy high-impact plastic. Figures not incl.
48 G 24715—Ship. wt. 1 lb. 5.99

366 ALL   Not recommended for children under 3.

D Superheroes™ meet Monsters and Superfoes in a fight to the finish! And only your imagination can set the limit on the fun you can have! 8-inch tall fully poseable figures dressed in authentic outfits, and ready for action! Ship. wt. 5 oz. each.

Superheroes and Superfoes. . . . . .each 3.29
48 G 24424—Superman   48 G 24425—Batman
48 G 24504—Spiderman   48 G 24426—Robin
48 G 24540—Shazam   48 G 24508—Joker
48 G 24690—Lizard   48 G 24691—Green Goblin

Mad Monsters. *Please state item number wanted.*
L 48 G 24592 D—Ship. wt. 2 oz. each. 3.29

01—Frankenstein   04—Wolfman
02—Dracula   05—Phantom of the Opera
03—Mummy   06—Hunchback of Notre Dame

SAVE $2—Buy any 3 monsters for only. 7.87

E Exploding Bridge with Batmobile and Batman. Recreate an exciting adventure between the Dynamic Duo and their arch enemy, Joker, with this action-packed playset. Press the Activator to "explode" bridge—but don't worry, you can put it back together again. Bridge, car, activator and 3½-inch high Batman figure included.
48 G 24121—Ship. wt. 1 lb. 14 oz. 10.99

Add Robin and Joker figures for more fun!
48 G 24565—Figures 3½ in. high. Wt. 3 oz..set **2.49**

F Hall of Justice™ is headquarters for your team of action heroes. Place 8-in. high figure in Translocation chamber and dial a disaster on the console. Poof! Hero is instantly translocated to the scene of the crime. Durable plastic playcase (21½x 10¾ in.) with fully detailed interior, map table. Figures not included.
48 G 24717—Ship. wt. 3 lbs. 12 oz. 14.94

World's Greatest Super Heroes: Montgomery Wards 1976 Christmas catalog showing some of the Mego Super Heroes and their accessories, including an Isis figure that was billed as exclusive to Montgomery Wards. After 1976 Isis was available at other department stores as well, such as Sears and J.C. Penneys.

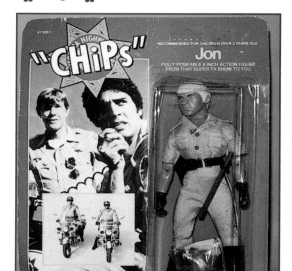

CHiPS: 8" dolls portraying the characters from the television series *CHiPS* were made from 1978 through 1981. The characters included Jon, Sarge, and Ponch. Shown in the photo is Jon. MOC: **$30.00 – 45.00.** *Courtesy Robin Englehart, vintagelane.com, photo by Nancy Jean Mong.*

Mermaid Doll Co.

Mermaid Doll (name unknown): This blond mermaid doll is 22" tall with sleep blue eyes, rooted lashes, and a twist waist. Her tail fin is blue. She is marked on her back "MERMAID DOLL CO./19©65." It is unknown if the top she is wearing is original. **$20.00 – 25.00.** *Courtesy Robin Englehart, vintagelane.com, photo by Nancy Jean Mong.*

Mermaid Doll (name unknown): 22" brunette mermaid doll with red tail fin. It is unknown if the clothing she has on is original. She has the same markings as doll on left. **$20.00 – 25.00.** *Courtesy Ann Wagner.*

Linda Williams: The brunette doll on the right represents Angela Cartwright as Linda Williams in the Danny Thomas television show *Make Room for Daddy.* The 14½" Linda Williams doll was sold extensively and is easily found on the collectors' market today. In 1959, Post Toasties advertised a $2.00 mail-in offer for this doll. While the 14½" Linda Williams doll is common, other less common dolls made in Angela Cartwright's image include a 20" and a 30" walker doll. The 14½" Linda Williams doll is marked "Linda Williams" on the back of her head. The doll has blue sleep eyes, even though the real Angel Cartwright had brown eyes. The orange hair doll in the photo is Dolly Ann and used the same mold as the Linda Williams doll. She is unmarked however the original mold markings of "Linda Williams" had been scratched out but can still be faintly detected on the back of her head. She has bright green eyes and freckles. Linda Williams: **$20.00 – 25.00.** Dolly Ann: **$15.00 – 20.00.** *Courtesy Ann Wagner.*

Angela Cartwright: 20" doll with olive green sleep eyes and four painted teeth. The doll is a walk-with-me doll. If she is held by her left hand and walked slowly, one leg will move in front of the other as if walking. The doll in the photograph is not wearing her original outfit. She is marked "Angela" on the back of her neck. Re-dressed: **$20.00 – 35.00.** *Courtesy Ann Wagner.*

Happy Hippies: 2½" doll that has a metal loop on top of his head and originally came with a silver chain so he could be worn as a necklace. His original paper tag reads "Happy Hippies" on one side and "©PARIS & CO./1968/MADE IN HONG KONG" on the other. Happy Hippies came in several different styles. **$20.00 – 25.00.**
Courtesy Robin Englehart, vintagelane.com, photo by Nancy Jean Mong.

Playskool

Dressy Bessy/Dapper Dan: Children growing up in the 1970s might remember two dolls that they used to help them learn how to button, buckle, snap, zip, lace, and tie: Dressy Bessy and Dapper. Over the years there were many different versions and sizes of these two dolls. On the left in the photo is Dapper Dan. He is 18" tall. Inside his buttoned shirt he has a vinyl vest with snaps, pants with a zipper, and a belt that buckles. On his feet are shoes with laces to tie. He is tagged "Dapper Dan/TEACHING DOLL/©PLAYSKOOL INC.,/CHICAGO, ILLINOIS/MADE IN HONG KONG" on one side and "PLAYSKOOL INC./A DIVISION OF MILTON BRADLEY CO/ALL NEW MATERIALS/STUFFED WITH 100% NEW POLYESTER FIBER" on the other. In the center of the photo is a smaller and more simplified version of Dapper Dan. This doll is 10½" tall and has painted eyes rather than button eyes. Inside his button vest he has a belt that buckles

and a zipper that zips. His shoes also tie. The small Dapper Dan in the photo is untagged but the tag may have come off. On the right is 18" Dressy Bessy. The doll in the photo is missing her yarn pigtails with ribbons. Inside her button vest she has a belt that snaps, another vest that ties, and a pocket that zips. Her shoes have laces to tie. She is tagged "Dressy Bessy/TEACHING DOLL/©1970 Playskool Inc. Under Berne &/Universal Copyright Convention/CHICAGO, ILLINOIS/MADE IN HONG KONG" on one side and "PLAYSKOOL INC./A DIVISION OF MILTON BRADLEY CO/ALL NEW MATERIALS/STUFFED WITH 100% NEW POLYESTER FIBER" on the other. These cloth dolls were used extensively by children so they are often found dirty and torn. Values are for lightly played with dolls. Mint condition dolls would command higher prices. Large Dressy Bessy/Dapper Dan: **$15.00 – 20.00.** Small Dapper Dan: **$10.00 – 15.00.**

P.M. Sales

Little information could be found or verified about the P.M. Sales Company. Several dolls marked P.M. Sales also have other company markings on them or on their original box which might mean P.M. Sales made dolls and distributed them to a variety of companies. The markings vary on P.M. Sales dolls, but many of them have a distinguishing mod look to them with heavy eye shadow and/or thick eyeliner in the corners of their eyes. The majority of PM Sales dolls are marked either 1965 or 1966.

Go Go Doll: 18" doll with rooted hair and sleep eyes. She is marked "27 EYE/NEW/S.M./A E 2/P.M. SALES INC/©1966" on the back of her neck and on the buttocks, "EA" with the two letters connected and the E written backwards. **$15.00 – 20.00.** *Courtesy Robin Englehart, vintagelane.com, photo by Nancy Jean Mong.*

Princess Grace Doll, Inc.

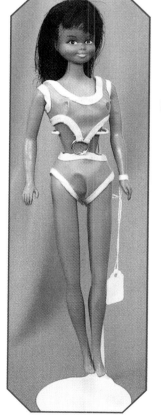

Princess Grace Doll: 11½" doll with rooted eyelashes and twist waist. The doll is marked "©1968/PRINCESS GRACE DOLL INC./HONG KONG." These cheaply made dolls often turn up in the white version, but very few black dolls have been spotted. The doll in the photo is wearing her original swimsuit. **$15.00 – 20.00.**

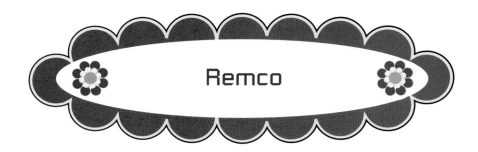

Remco

The Littlechap Family: The Littlechap family of dolls first appeared on the market in 1964. Their biography, which appeared in their fashion booklets and clothing boxes, described them as an upscale American family consisting of the golf-loving father Dr. John; his president-of-the-PTA wife Lisa; their daughter, 17 year-old-honor-student Judy; and their 10 year-old tomboy daughter Libby. Their excellent quality fashions were made in Japan and included many detailed accessories. John Littlechap originally came dressed in a terry cloth robe with a towel around his neck and the three female members of the family came wearing terry cloth wraps. Since the Littlechap dolls were odd sizes, it was difficult for them to share clothing with other fashion dolls on the market at the time, thus creating the need for consumers to purchase Remco Littlechap clothing made specifically for them. Each Littlechap doll is marked with his or her name and "REMCO INDUSTRIES/1963©" in a circle on his or her back.

The origin of the set of Littlechap dolls shown in the photo is unknown, but it is possible these fully dressed dolls could have been used as a store display by a retailer. The dolls have been hand stitched on a cardboard backing and are each dressed in one or two outfits. The cardboard backing might be the original backing from the rare four-doll Littlechap set of dolls, all who originally came dressed in their terry cloth robes or wraps. It is possible a store owner may have used the dolls from the four-doll set and dressed them up for display before restitching them back onto the cardboard. No other sets of fully dressed Littlechaps like this one have been seen previously to use for comparison to determine value but based on the dolls and clothing priced alone, the set would be estimated to be in the $500.00 price range.

Dr. John and Lisa Littlechap: Here are Dr. John Littlechap and his wife Lisa. They are wearing outfits sold separately for them, John's Tuxedo and Lisa's Basic Black Dress. Loose dolls wearing mint and complete outfits: **$40.00 – 55.00 each.**

Dr. John Littlechap: Close-up of the trophy in Dr. John's Golf Outfit.

Dr. John Littlechap: Dr. John's Golf Outfit. The sweater in the outfit is different than the one shown in the Littlechap's fashion booklet. NRFP: **$25.00 – 40.00.**

Lisa Littlechap: Lisa's White Two-Piece Dress. NRFP: **$25.00 – 40.00.**

Lisa Littlechap: Lisa's Fur-Trimmed Suede Coat. NRFP: **$25.00 – 40.00.**

Judy Littlechap: Judy's Party Dress. NRFP: **$25.00 – 40.00.**

Libby Littlechap: Libby's Three-Piece Blazer Outfit. NRFP: **$25.00 – 40.00.**

Winking Heidi: 5½" Heidi was the main character in Remco's line of Pocketbook dolls. She has a slightly out-of-proportion sized head and a button on her stomach that when pushed springs her hand up to wave. She came housed in a red plastic pocketbook-style case. A later version of Heidi was Winking Heidi. This doll came in a cardboard box and had open and shut eyes, unlike the original issue doll which had painted eyes. When the button on Winking Heidi's stomach is pressed she winks her eye. MIB: **$45.00 – 55.00.** *Courtesy Hillary and Cliff James, Toy With Me.*

Winking Heidi: Winking Heidi out of her box. The doll is marked "404/REMCO IND. INC./©1968/K" on her head and "©/REMCO/ INDUSTRIES/ INC." on her back. Loose doll: **$15.00 – 20.00.**

Only Sears has
a **Heidi** that
GROWS UP

$**3**99

grows from this

to a big girl like this

First she's a sweet young thing in her play clothes and then—presto!—she changes into a swinging little miss in a party dress. You won't believe your eyes . . she actually grows taller from 6¼ inches to 7½ inches. She has 2 complete outfits and 2 different hair styles. Just extend her body . . switch clothes, wig and she's a whole new doll. Plastic. Shipping wt. 10 oz.
49 N 30286 . . . $3.99

MINIATURE DOLLS

Poseable Tiny Teen with trunk of clothes

Tiny Teen is a real fashion plate. She likes to change so often that she travels with a plastic steamer trunk with 6 outfits on real hangers and a dresser. She has rooted hair that can be combed . . even has eyelashes. Wired vinyl body is completely bendable. 5 inches tall. Shipping wt. 11 oz.
49N30274. Set $4.99

$**4**99

Pee Wees and their trunk of clothes

Two wee vinyl tots to dress in so many outfits . . each one has 3 extra outfits. And Baby Pee Wee drinks and wets. They fit in their own plastic steamer trunk that's complete with a dresser and real hangers. You can brush and comb their rooted hair. Dolls are 4 in. tall with one-piece body and turning head. Shipping wt. 12 oz.
49N30273. Set $4.99

$**4**99

Now you can get a winking Heidi

Pocketbook Heidi waves "Hi" or "Bye"

$**3**49

$**2**49

Something new has been added to tiny Heidi's charms . . her eyes open and close and when you push her 'magic' button she winks. Soft jointed vinyl body . . rooted hair to comb. 5½ in. tall. Dressed in colorful outfit. Shpg. wt. 5 oz.
49 N 30146 . . . . $3.49

She loves to go visiting with you . . just pop her into the pocketbook case—room for your hanky and coin purse too. Soft jointed vinyl body . . rooted hair to comb. 5½ in. tall. In pert jumper and blouse. Push her button to make her wave.
49N3999—Wt. 10 oz..$2.49

$**1**99

Fold away vinyl Shanty Shack with Troll

Two rooms furnished, to suit this 3-in. troll. Uniquely designed bedroom and living room down to the authentic tree-stump table and chairs. All furnishings colorfully vacuum formed. Vinyl troll has real sheepskin hair. Carry case 10x8x9 in. high.
49 N 30275—Shipping weight 2 pounds 10 ounces . . . Set $1.99

Carry case Playhouse for your tiniest dolls

$**4**97

Two full stories give lots of play room for Heidi, Pee Wee or any 4 to 6-in. dolls. Mediterranean styling screened onto vinyl house inside and out. First floor den has chair, table, TV and opens onto patio walk. Upstairs bedroom and baby nursery . . just perfect for a Baby Pee Wee. House closes to 13x9x7½ in. high. Carrying handle.
49 N 9257—Shpg. wt. 3 lbs..$4.97

Heidi Grows Up: This Sears exclusive Heidi went from a young girl to a sophisticated young lady. The author has never seen a Heidi Grows Up doll to know for sure if this doll was actually marketed. The clothing and grown up wig she is wearing in the catalog picture are very similar to the ones shown on Growing Sally, another Remco doll that grew up. Not enough examples to determine a fair market value. *1968 Sears Christmas Catalog.*

> ### Growing Sally 3^{95} seen on TV
>
> 5 You can make Sally grow from tot to teen in just a few seconds—any time you want to! She changes from red headed cutie to platinum haired beauty because she comes with two wigs. Play dress, formal and shoes included. She's abt. 5½ in. tall as a little girl, grows to teen abt. 7 in. tall. She's made of vinyl and is fully jointed. Extra outfits for Sally are sold below.
> 48 T 10260—Ship. wt. 11 oz. . . . . Growing Sally 3.95
>
> 6 Extra play dress, ball gown and shoes for Sally.
> 48 T 10763—Ship. wt. 8 oz. . . . . outfits 1.88
>
> ## SAVE THIS CATALOG!
> Order toys until August 31, 1969.

She grows!

Growing Sally: 5½" doll that can be stretched to grow to 7". The bald-headed doll came with two wigs: one styled in pigtails, the other in an upswept hairdo. She came with a short play dress and a pink gown and the idea was to have Sally change from a young girl to a lovely young lady. Growing Sally was also issued in a black version. This picture from Montgomery Wards 1968 Christmas catalog shows Growing Sally with her two wigs and two outfits, as well as a pair of outfits which could be purchased separately.

Growing Sally: Growing Sally shown in her original box. The mini dress she is wearing is different from the one shown in the 1968 Montgomery Wards catalog. NRFB: **$40.00 – 45.00.** *Courtesy Michele Casino.*

Billy: This is Heidi's little brother Billy. Although shown in the Sears 1966 Christmas catalog, prior to locating the doll in the photo the author had not believed he had actually been manufactured. He is extremely rare. The doll in the photo is missing his original hat, boots, and scarf. Loose/no case: **$30.00 – 45.00.**

Trav-A-Long House for all little dolls

A SEARS EXCLUSIVE $3⁸⁹

Two full stories give lots of play room for Heidi, Jan, Pee Wee, or any 4 to 6-inch dolls. Lifelike details and realistic room scenes are screened onto the vinyl house both inside and out. First floor kitchen has a tiny oven and hideaway table and chair. There's a studio couch in the den. Upstairs bedroom has a bed, night table, chest of drawers. Folds to 13x9x7½ inches high. Dolls not included.
49N9345—Wt. 3 lbs. 4 oz.$3.89

Heidi's Accessories

3-outfit Wardrobe will make Heidi the best-dressed little doll on the block. Whether her day will be dress up or play, she has just the right fashion for it. Each dress is smartly-styled of cotton and has color-cued panties and cute little plastic shoes.
49 N 3978—Wt. 4 oz. Set $1.69

Hats 'n Dresses . . 3 stylish little outfits for Heidi and Jan to switch and wear. The latest "mod" fashions include a Mondrian shift with pillbox topper; a low-slung hip-hugger and cute skimmer hat; an A-line polka dot dress with a natty sailor bonnet.
49 N 3961—Wt. 4 oz.....$1.99

Bedroom Set . . great fun for a pajama party! Double bunk bed with ladder, spreads bolsters, even a tiny poodle. The dresser has drawers you can open and a real mirror. At bedtime, switch the lamp off! Order one "AA" battery from page 482.
49 N 9364—Wt. 1 lb. 8 oz. $3.69

Pretty pink Jeep takes her on her merry way with a cute little poodle for company. Handy outdoor phone booth. Tiny parking meter really works . . you even get a make-believe coin to put in the meter. All in plastic.
49 N 9398—Wt. 1 lb. 4 oz.$1.99

Magic House-n-Garden. Watch with Heidi as real grass and "bushes" grow in the garden . . all you do is plant magic seeds. Not messy, and it's fun to rake, hoe and cut the grass with tiny garden tools. Cottage has window boxes to plant, too. Inside there's an easy chair, sofa-bed. Sturdy metal, plastic. 38 in. long. Unassembled.
79 N 9366C—Wt. 5 lbs..$10.99

Backyard Swing Set. Suzy loves to be pushed on the swing or down the slide. There's a seesaw, pail, shovel and ball. Plastic, 13 in. long.Wt. 3 lbs.
79 N 9225C.....$2.79

3-outfit Dress-up Wardrobe fits Suzy and all your other 7 to 8-in. dolls. Sacque, matching blanket, dress, panties, coat, bonnet, rattle, bracelet. Shipping weight 4 ounces.
49 N 3212...........$1.99

HEIDI

. . the friendly Pocketbook Doll

. . press the magic button and she waves good-by

and here's Jan
. . just like Heidi, she has her own carry-case and gives a cheery wave

2 $2⁵⁹

1 Heidi's 5½ in. tall and a pocketbook full of fun. She wears a plaid jumper and white blouse. You can comb her pretty blond hair and move her plastic arms and legs.
49 N 3999—Shpg. wt. 14 oz. $2.59

2 Jan is Japanese and wears a charming oriental dress. She can wear and do everything Heidi does.
49 N 3959—Shpg. wt. 14 oz. $2.59

1 $2⁵⁹

Meet Heidi's little sis and brother . .

Hildy and Billy

A tiny pair so little, so lovable, so lifelike! Hildy has shiny blond hair that you can comb and wears a bright little striped dress. Billy wears long pants, sweater and cap and has a jaunty scarf knotted at his neck. Both twins are 4½ in. high, are made of plastic, and have movable arms and legs.

Like everything else in Sears books, it's so easy to order by phone. Shipping weight 5 ounces.
49 N 3960–Set $3.49

$3⁴⁹ Set

Suzy Cute . . loves to be cuddled . . press her tummy, she lifts her arms

$2¹⁹ Doll and Crib

She's 7½ in. tall and all dressed in blue. Give Suzy her bottle but don't go away . . won't you change her wet diaper? Move her soft plastic head, arms, legs. Comb her rooted Saran hair. Flip her mattress, give her the rattle to play with . . soon she'll be napping . . s-s-h-h-h, don't wake the baby! Shpg. wt. 2 lbs. 4 oz.
49 N 3156.........$2.19

BKMG **Sears** 615

Heidi and Friends: Sears 1966 Christmas catalog advertising Heidi and her friends and accessories, including her little sister and brother Hildy and Billy. The catalog indicates that the two dolls were sold as a set. Hildy was also sold separately for several years, but it is unknown if Billy was ever sold alone or if he was only available this one year in a set with Hildy.

196

Hildy, Billy, and Herby: The doll on the left is Heidi's little sister Hildy, in the center is her seldom-seen brother Billy, and on the right is Heidi's little brother Herby. All three dolls are made from the same head and body molds. Hildy and Herby with original clothing and carrying cases: **$30.00 – 55.00 each.** Billy loose/no case: **$30.00 – 45.00.**

Heidi/Spunky 3-in-One Bowling Set: This 1967 set was sold for Heidi, Jan, Spunky, and all the Remco Pocketbook dolls. The set is called Spunky 3-in-One Bowling, but the instruction sheet and the labels on the toy itself read "Heidi 3-in-One Bowling." The set allows Remco's Pocketbook dolls to bowl, play skee ball, and play shuffleboard. MIB: **$25.00 – 35.00.** *Courtesy Robin Englehart, vintagelane.com, photo by Nancy Jean Mong.*

T.V. Jones and Pussy Meow: These 5¾" dolls came packaged inside television shaped cases. Both T.V. Jones and Pussy Meow had buttons on their chests that when pushed caused the dolls to turn their heads. Both animals also make a little squeak noise like a bark and a meow when their button is pushed. The two dolls are shown with T.V. Jones's chair and bed, both very rare. Other characters in the line included Hana Hippo, Ellie Elephant, Patsy Panda, and Mr. and Mrs. Mouse. T.V. Jones in case: **$75.00 – 100.00.** Loose T.V. Jones: **$25.00 – 40.00.** Pussy Meow in case: **$80.00 – 110.00.** Loose Pussy Meow: **$25.00 – 40.00.** Furniture: **$45.00 – 75.00 each.** *Courtesy Jennie Brott.*

Pussy Meow: Both T.V. Jones and Pussy Meow had outfits that could be purchased separately for them. The Pussy Meow ensemble in the photo is called Secret Agent Outfit. NRFP: **$30.00 – 45.00.** *Courtesy Robin Englehart, vintagelane.com, photo by Nancy Jean Mong.*

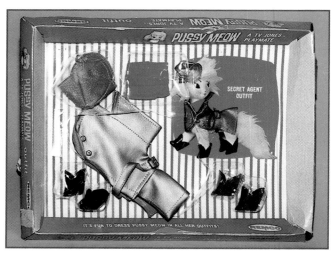

Hana Hippo: From Remco's T.V. Jones line comes his playmate Hana Hippo. She is 5½" tall. She is marked "Remco Ind. 1966." She has been found with either pink or blue hair, and since the doll on the box shows Hana with white hair, it's possible she was issued with that hair color as well. Hana is extremely hard to find. MIB: **$125.00 – 200.00.** *Courtesy Jennie Brott.*

Hana Hippo: Like all the T.V. Jones playmates, Hanna had outfits that could be purchased separately. From left to right in the photo are Style 4080 Sleep Set, Style 4075 Winter Set, Style 4083 Rain Set, and Style 4084 Nurse Set. The fashions also fit friends Ellie Elephant and Patsy Panda. NRFP: **$20.00 – 30.00 each.** *Courtesy Robin Englehart, vintagelane.com, photo by Nancy Jean Mong.*

Mr. And Mrs. Mouse House: Also playmates of T.V. Jones were Remco's Mr. and Mrs. Mouse. Both mice are vinyl with jointed arms and legs. Mr. Mouse has black hair and comes wearing a red flannel nightshirt with his name on it along with a red flannel stocking nightcap. Mrs. Mouse has red hair and comes wearing a red flannel nightgown with her name on it along with a red flannel nightcap. At least one extra outfit set was sold separately for them. The two dolls came in a plastic house with a set of bunk beds, a table, and two chairs. The 4¾" dolls are marked "REMCO/©1966" on their neck. House with mice: **$175.00 – 225.00.** *Courtesy Michele Casino.*

199

Elly and Andy Tree House: Remco's Mr. And Mrs. Mouse had twin children named Elly and Andy. 3" Elly and Andy came with a tree house with a working elevator. The tree house playset included a china cabinet, a chest with pull-out drawer (for overnight mouse guests), two brown chairs, a brown table with a decal on top, and a triangular slice of cheese. The plastic furniture has been found in both red or yellow. Not shown in the photo is a swing that hung from the side branch. All the Mouse family members and their accessories are rare, but Elly and Andy and their tree house are harder to find then their parents with their house. Tree house with mice: **$200.00 – 350.00.** *Courtesy Michele Casino.*

Li'l Winking Herby Hippy: 16" doll has a button on his stomach that allows him to wink his right eye. Herby is marked "REMCO, INC./19©68" on his head. **$30.00 – 45.00.** *Courtesy Elaine McGrath.*

Li'l Winking Herby Hippy: This Li'l Winking Herby Hippy has different clothing from that shown on page 200. His necklace is different as well. He comes with sandals, but all the other Herbys the author has seen were found with bare feet. **$30.00 – 45.00.**

Tippy Tumbles: 17" doll that does somersaults and handstands with the aid of a plastic pocketbook battery case that attaches by a cord to a plug in her ankle. Tippy is marked "SM/E51/ REMCO IND.INC./19©69." MIB: **$35.00 – 40.00.** *Courtesy Robin Englehart, vintagelane.com, photo by Nancy Jean Mong.*

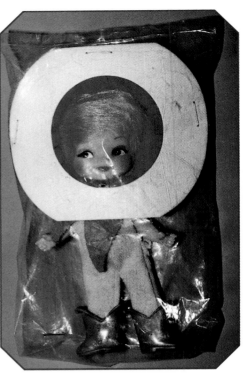

Finger Ding Flower Kids: Finger Ding Flower Kids were Finger Ding dolls wearing flower petal hats and leaf-shaped collars. All the Finger Ding line of dolls had no legs, only a head, torso, and arms and a pair of tights that children inserted their fingers in to form the legs of the dolls. The Flower Kid dolls included Li'l Buttercup, Li'l Daisy, and Li'l Rose. Shown in the photo are Li'l Rose and Li'l Daisy in their original packages. The 5" Finger Ding Flower Kids are marked "2504/REMCO IND.INC./19©66" on their heads and "©1969/REMCO IND. INC./U.S. & FOREIGN/PAT. PEND./HONG KONG" on their backs. MIP: **$35.00 – 65.00.** *Courtesy Michele Casino.*

Finger Ding Flower Kids: Here is Li'l Rose shown in a plastic bag. Towards the end of a line, it was common practice for manufacturers to use up old stock by packaging dolls in inexpensive plastic bags rather than boxes or other more expensive packaging. Dolls in bags were often used for mail-away offers or premiums as well. It's unknown if the doll in the photo was sold in this bag as a premium or as left over stock. MIP: **$20.00 – 30.00.** *Courtesy Robin Englehart, vintagelane.com, photo by Nancy Jean Mong.*

Finger Ding Animals: There are three Finger Ding Animals including Hildy Hen, who came with her own plastic egg, Spunky Monkey, who came with plastic roller skates, and Kitty Kangaroo. Kitty is shown in the photo along with her baby Joey in her pouch. The baby pops his head out when Kitty's tail is moved. Kitty is marked "REMCO IND. INC./ 19©70" on her back. Loose with feet: **$35.00 – 50.00.** *Courtesy Michele Casino.*

Hug-a-Bug: 4" doll with plastic wings and a clip so that children could attach it to their clothing. Often the wings are missing. These little dolls are difficult to find due to their small size and many people not recognizing them as an item collectors would treasure. Hug-A-Bugs are marked "Remco 1971" on their wings. **$35.00 – 50.00.** *Courtesy Michele Casino.*

Flintstones Finger Dings: Pebbles, Dino, and Fred Flintstone Finger Ding dolls, circa 1970. These Finger Ding dolls are very hard to find. **$50.00 – 60.00 each.** *Courtesy Michele Casino.*

Laurie Partridge: Doll representing Susan Dey as Laurie Partridge from the Partridge Family. The 19" doll has a vinyl head, arms, and legs, and a plastic torso. Laurie is marked on her neck "HONG KONG, REMCO INC. 1973." MIB: **$450.00 – 525.00.** *Courtesy Michele Casino.*

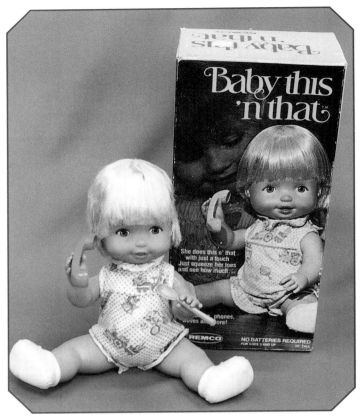

Baby This 'n That: This 13" doll was available both in white and black versions. Baby This 'n That came with small accessories to hold in her hand including a phone, toothbrush, and a spoon. When one or both of her feet are squeezed, her arms move, her hands rotate, or her mouth moves as if eating. The doll is marked "MADE IN HONG KONG" on the back of her head under her hairline, "©REMCO 1970/N.Y.N.Y. 10010" on her head, and "©1976 REMCO TOYS/NEW YORK, N.Y. 10010/MADE IN HONG KONG/PRO" on her back. MIB: **$35.00 – 45.00.**

I Dream of Jeannie: This 6½" doll was released to correspond with the Hanna Barbera animated cartoon of Jeannie that was part of the The Fred Flintstone and Friends cartoon show and not the 1960s television show *I Dream of Jeannie* starring Barbara Eden. The doll has posing vinyl legs with a wire inside. There is a copyright date of 1977 on the back of the box. MIB: **$65.00 – 100.00.** *Courtesy Robin Englehart, vintagelane.com, photo by Nancy Jean Mong.*

I Dream of Jeannie: Back of Jeannie's box showing some of her fashions. MIB: **$65.00 – 100.00.** *Courtesy Robin Englehart, vintagelane.com, photo by Nancy Jean Mong.*

I Dream of Jeannie Dream Bottle: This bottle playset came with a Jeannie doll slightly different from the boxed doll shown in the previous photo. The doll that came with the bottle playset has hard plastic legs with jointed knees, unlike the boxed doll shown above with vinyl posing legs. The doll in the playset came dressed in pink, while the doll sold separately came wearing blue. MIB playset with doll: **$200.00 – 225.00.** *Courtesy Michele Casino.*

A division of Operation Bootstrap, Inc., Shindana was primarily known for their black dolls in the 1970s. Their line of dolls included a number of black celebrity dolls.

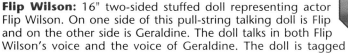

Shindana

Flip Wilson: 16" two-sided stuffed doll representing actor Flip Wilson. On one side of this pull-string talking doll is Flip and on the other side is Geraldine. The doll talks in both Flip Wilson's voice and the voice of Geraldine. The doll is tagged "1970 Street Corner Productions, Inc./Operation Bootstrap, Inc./Los Angeles, Calif. 90001/Commonwealth of Pennsylvania Department of Labor and Industry/Stuffed Toys Registration Number/211 APPROVED." Mute: **$25.00 – 40.00.** MIB: **$75.00 – 100.00.** *Courtesy Robin Englehart, vintagelane.com, photo by Nancy Jean Mong.*

Li'l Souls: These 6" or 9" all-cloth dolls came out around 1971. The 6" dolls included Natra and Coochy. The 9" Li'l Souls included Sis and Wilky. Each doll came with a story coloring book. Shown in the photo on the left is 6" Natra in her original box. NRFB: **$35.00 – 55.00.** *Courtesy Robin Englehart, vintagelane.com.*

Li'l Souls: 6" Li'l Souls Coochy. **$15.00 – 20.00.** *Courtesy Robin Englehart, vintagelane.com.*

Li'l Souls Wilky: 9" Li'l Souls Wilky in his original box. NRFB: **$45.00 – 55.00.**

Li'l Souls Wilky: The 9" doll is tagged "Li'l Souls™/ ©Shindana Toys/ Div. Of Operation/Bootstrap, Inc./L.A. California/Made in Hong Kong" along with material content. **$15.00 – 20.00.** *Courtesy Robin Englehart, vintagelane.com.*

Li'l Souls Sis: The 9" doll is tagged the same as Wilky, "Li'l Souls™/©Shindana Toys/Div. Of Operation/Bootstrap, Inc./L.A. California/Made in Hong Kong" along with material content. Loose doll: **$15.00 – 20.00.** *Courtesy Robin Englehart, vintagelane.com.*

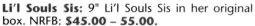

Li'l Souls Sis: 9" Li'l Souls Sis in her original box. NRFB: **$45.00 – 55.00.**

Julius (Dr. J.) Erving: 9½" doll made in the image of basketball hero, Julius Erving. The doll is marked "SHINDANA TOYS/©1977" on his head, and "HONG KONG" on his body. MIB: **$95.00 – 125.00.** *Courtesy Sharon Criscione.*

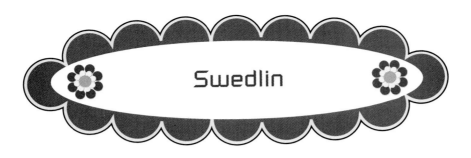

Swedlin

Mini Martians: These 1967 Sears exclusive figures are popular with many collectors and are very hard to find. The vinyl Mini Martians are 4½" inches tall. They are marked "J. SWEDLIN, INC.1967/MADE IN JAPAN" on the back of their necks. The Mini Martians included Professor Pook, Marti, Mini, Bonnie, Meri, and Teenie. Additional outfits and accessories were sold for the Mini Martians. From left to right in photo are Bonnie dressed in her original Lunar Sarong, Professor Pook in his original outfit, Marti standing in the ultra rare Mini Martians spaceship wearing Jet Jumper, Mini in her original Silver Cape, and Bonnie in Zoom Suit. The space ship originally had a plastic dome over the top. All original: **$50.00 – 75.00 each.** Spaceship: **$100.00 – 150.00.** *Courtesy Lisa Petrucci.*

Mini Martians: From left to right in photo are Marti in Jet Jumper, Meri in Solar Shift, Bonnie in Lunar Sarong, Professor Pook in his original outfit, Bonnie in Zoom Suit, and Mini in Silver Cape. All original: **$50.00 – 75.00 each.** *Courtesy Lisa Petrucci.*

Mini Martians: From left to right are Mini wearing Stellar Shift, Bonnie wearing Galaxy Garb, and Teenie wearing Bonnie's original Lunar Sarong. Hair ribbons not original. **$50.00 – 75.00 each.** *Courtesy Jennie Brott.*

Mini Martians: Shown in the photo is Bonnie, minus her original outfit. Dolls nude or re-dressed: **$40.00 – 45.00 each.**

Mini Martians: Sears 1967 Christmas Catalog showing their exclusive Mini Martians and their outfits and accessories.

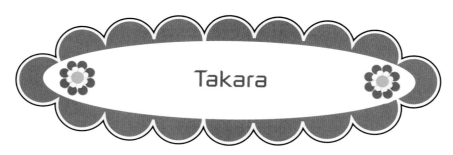

Takara

Chi-Chan Carrying Case: Takara made many dolls and toys for the Japanese market. Chi-Chan was one of Takara's popular tiny dolls that was a little over 3" tall. Beginning in 1969, Chi-Chan was sold as one of the Chibikko mates (Chibikko means little in Japanese). Chi-Chan has two sisters, her older sister is Kei-Chan, and her younger sister had no name but was just called Aka-Chan — which means baby in Japanese. She also has some dark-skinned friends named Peanuts-Nuts-Chan, Coconut-Coco-Chan, and Almond-Amo-Chan, and they came from a tropical island. These dolls were called Kuro-Chan Mates (Kuro means black). Many vinyl cases and play structures were made for Chi-Chan and her family and friends, including the case shown in the photo. **$40.00 – 65.00.** *Courtesy Jennie Brott.*

Timely Toys

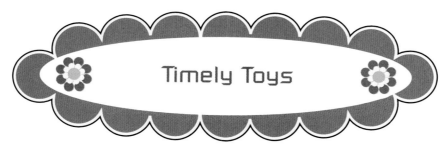

Tweenys: 1967 Going to School set. The dolls are similar to Uneeda's Pee Wee dolls. MIB: **$15.00 – 20.00.** *Courtesy Robin Englehart, vintagelane.com, photo by Nancy Jean Mong.*

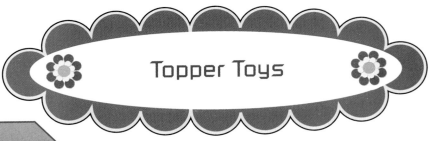

Dawn: 6½" Dawn and her friends were quite popular from 1970 through 1973. Over 30 dolls and close to 100 outfits were offered in the Dawn line. A common problem with Dawn dolls is green discoloration around their knees from the metal inside reacting to the vinyl. This problem occurs even on NRFB dolls. In the case of NRFB dolls, if the doll is dressed in an outfit that covers the green, the discoloration shouldn't affect the value much as it is so common. Those NRFB dolls dressed in mini dresses where the green is very visible are valued slightly lower than those without it. Loose dolls with green knees are usually valued around **$5.00 – 20.00** depending on the doll. In the photo is the standard Dawn doll wearing her original outfit. **$10.00 – 20.00.**

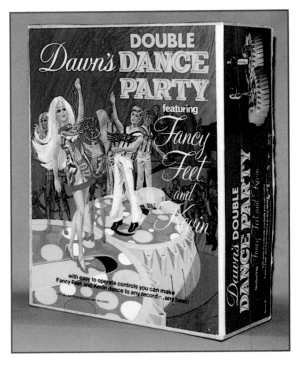

Dawn's Double Dance Party featuring Fancy Feet and Kevin: Platinum blond Fancy Feet and blond molded-hair Kevin were two dolls in the Dawn line that were only available with Dawn's Dance Party playsets. The three playsets they came in were Dawn's Dance Party featuring Fancy Feet, Dawn's Dance Party featuring Kevin and Dawn's Double Dance Party featuring Fancy Feet and Kevin. MIB: **$65.00 – 100.00.**
Courtesy Robin Englehart, vintagelane.com, photo by Nancy Jean Mong.

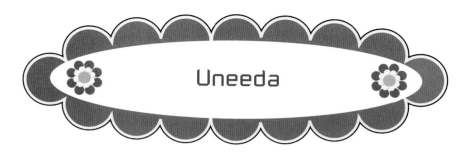

Dollikin: The fully-jointed 21" hard-plastic Dollikin dolls came out in the late 1950s but continued to be offered into the early 1960s. In the 1970s vinyl and plastic Dollikin dolls were made in 11½" and 6½" sizes but are not nearly as popular with collectors as the earlier 21" hard plastic dolls. The 21" Dollikin dolls came with different hair styles and colors, and a large variety of outfits. The doll shown in the photo is all original in her original box. MIB: **$375.00 – 550.00.** *Courtesy Hillary and Cliff James, Toy With Me.*

Dollikin: In 1970 an 11½" Dollikin doll was introduced. These Dollikin dolls came in blond, brunette, black, and red hair colors and are jointed at the shoulder, elbow, wrist, thigh, knee, and foot. Dollikin dolls are marked "©UNEEDA DOLL CO. INC./MCMLX1X/ MADE IN HONG KONG" on their heads and "DOLLIKIN®/U.S. PAT. #3,010253/OTHER U.S. & FOR./ PAT.PEND." on their backs. The doll in the photo is wearing her original jumpsuit, and a scarf belt from another Dollikin doll. She is missing her original shoes. Doll missing shoes: **$10.00 – 15.00.**

Suzette: 11" Barbie-like fashion doll with exotic, slanted eyes. She is marked "N.F." on her neck and "©UNEEDA/DOLL CO./INC./1962" on her back. Previous to issuing this version of Suzette, Uneeda had another doll named Suzette who was 10" and was similar to Vogue's Jill doll. Loose, re-dressed: **$40.00 – 50.00.**

Petal People: This troll-like doll is 6½" tall and used the same body as Uneeda's Wishnik Trolls. The doll is marked "UNEEDA/19©64." on his head. Markings on his back read "UNEEDA/WISHNIK™/PAT.PEND./" and possibly a patent number (illegible). His box reads "As you collect them all hang your 'petals' on your wall." And "UNEEDA DOLL CO., INC./BROOKLYN, NEW YORK MADE IN U.S.A." MIB: **$20.00 – 25.00.**

Petal People: These 6½" troll-like dolls are a later issue of Petal People produced in the 1980s. Shown are Tulip, Daisy, and Daffodil. The dolls are marked "©UNEEDA DOLL CO." on their heads and "U.D. CO. INC./MCMLXXVII/MADE IN HONG KONG" on their backs. Although the dolls are marked with the date 1977, their boxes are dated 1983. Their box reads, "MCMLXXXIII, made in the British crown colony of Hong Kong." MIB: **$15.00 – 20.00 each.**

Tiny Teens: In 1967 Uneeda came out with a line of dolls called Tiny Teens which were 6" tall with rooted hair and rooted eyelashes. These dolls were similar to Hasbro's Dolly Darlings dolls. Some Tiny Teens were sold in clear plastic bubbles mounted on cardboard backings, and others were sold in boxes such as the one shown here. Tiny Teens are marked "© U.D. CO. INC. 1967/HONG KONG" on their heads and "© U.D. CO. INC./1967/MADE IN/HONG KONG" on their backs. Uneeda sold another fashion doll under the name Tinyteen from 1957 to 1960. These dolls were 10½" tall and were meant to compete with the popular selling 10½" Vogue Jill and 10½" Little Miss Revlon dolls which were out about the same time. While the names Tinyteen and Tiny Teens can cause confusion, there is no mistaking the late 1950s 10½" doll from the 6" mid-1960s dolls. MIB: **$25.00 – 30.00.**
Courtesy Robin Englehart, vintagelane.com, photo by Nancy Jean Mong.

L'il Agatha Bride: 9¾" doll with a vinyl head and lightweight plastic limbs and torso. Her box indicates she was copyright 1967. She is marked "HONG KONG" on her neck and back. Her dress is tagged "MADE IN HONG KONG." MIB: **$15.00 – 20.00.**

Little Sophisticates/Georgina: Uneeda put out a group of 8" poseable dolls called Little Sophisticates. They had closed eyes with blue eye shadow and long rooted eye lashes. In the photo is Georgina never removed from her card. Other Little Sophisticates included Penelope, Rosanna, Marika, Kristina, and Suzana. Uneeda also made Tiny Sophisticates that were 6". NRFP: **$45.00 – 55.00.** *Courtesy Robin Englehart, vintagelane.com, photo by Nancy Jean Mong.*

Little Sophisticates/Kristina: Uneeda's 8" Little Sophisticate Kristina. Loose doll: **$15.00 – 20.00.** *Courtesy Robin Englehart, vintagelane.com, photo by Nancy Jean Mong.*

Little Sophisticates: All six of the Little Sophisticates dolls wearing their original outfits. From left to right Georgina, Rosanna, Kristina, Marika, Suzana, and Penelope. The dolls were made in either Hong Kong or Japan. The dolls made in Japan are marked "UNEEDA DOLL CO. INC/1967/MADE IN JAPAN" on their heads and "©UNEEDA DOLL CO, INC/1967/MADE IN JAPAN" on their backs. Their clothing is tagged "LITTLE SOPHISTI-CATES/©UNEEDA DOLL CO., INC. 1967/MADE IN JAPAN." The dolls made in Hong Kong are marked "UNEEDA DOLL CO. INC./MCMLXVII/HONG KONG" on their heads and "©UNEEDA/DOLL CO. INC./MCMLXVII/MADE IN/HONG KONG" on their backs. Their clothing is tagged "MADE IN HONG KONG." **$15.00 – 20.00 each.**
Courtesy Karen Hickey.

Unknown Doll: 19½" doll with vinyl head and hard plastic body and limbs. Her side-glancing eyes have blue eye shadow above them. She is marked "Uneeda Doll Co., Inc./19©67/98." **$15.00 – 20.00.** *Courtesy Ann Wagner.*

Pee Wee: Pee Wee dolls were made by Uneeda starting in the mid-1960s and continuing into the 1980s. There was a large variety of the 3½" Pee Wee dolls sold over that time, sporting many different hairstyles, hair colors, and outfits. The earliest Pee Wee dolls are marked "Pee-Wees" on their feet, while later issues do not have the Pee Wee name on them. Because they were sold extensively, Pee Wee dolls are relatively easy to locate today. Vinyl cases, houses, or totes are not as common and are usually worth more than the dolls. Earlier Pee Wee dolls are marked "HONG KONG" on their backs and "PEE-WEES/T.M." on the bottom of their foot or "HONG KONG" on their heads and "PEE-WEES/©U.D.CO. INC./1965/HONG KONG" on their backs. Dolls in original clothing: **$5.00 – 10.00 each.** MIB: **$12.00 – 20.00.** Vinyl structures: **$15.00 – 30.00.** *Courtesy Robin Englehart, vintagelane.com, photo by Nancy Jean Mong.*

Pee Wee: This 3½" Pee Wee doll was called Dream Time. Other dolls listed on the back of her box are Dance Time, Nite Time, School Time, Nurse Time, Spring Time, Bride Time, Winter Time, Bikini Time, Flower Time, Garden Time, and Play Time. Dream Time Pee Wee is copyright 1965. MIB: **$15.00 – 20.00.**

Pee Wee: This 3½" Pee Wee doll is School Time. School Time Pee Wee's copyright date on her box is 1966. MIB: **$12.00 – 15.00.**

Pee Wee: 3½" Bikini Time Pee Wee doll, copyright 1966. MIB: **$12.00 – 15.00.**

Pee Wee: 3½" Bride Time Pee Wee.
MIB: **$15.00 – 20.00.** *Courtesy Robin Engle-hart, vintagelane.com, photo by Nancy Jean Mong.*

HeeWee: HeeWee dolls were the male version of Pee Wee dolls. They came dressed in all types of uniforms. In the photo is a cardboard store display of eight different HeeWee dolls dressed in their original outfits. HeeWee dolls are marked "1966/©U.D.CO,INC." on their heads, "U.D.CO./©/1965" on the bottom of their left foot and "PEE-WEES/T.M." on the bottom of their right foot. MOC display: **$50.00 – 100.00.** *Courtesy Karen Hickey.*

Pong: One of the Ping Pong series of dolls. The doll is 4" tall. Package is marked "MCMLXX1" (1971). MOC: **$10.00 – 15.00.** *Courtesy Robin Englehart, vintagelane.com, photo by Nancy Jean Mong.*

Baby Bumpkins: 11" drink and wet doll. Her box is dated MCXLXXII (1972). Mint with box: **$10.00 – 15.00.** *Courtesy Robin Englehart, vintagelane.com, photo by Nancy Jean Mong.*

Dana: 5½" doll with hair that grows longer. A grow hair strand on an elastic could be pulled out of the top of her head and slipped into a slot on her head to stay the length desired. When the hair is taken out of the slot, it goes shorter by springing back into her head. The back of Dana's box reads "Hi, I am going to tell you a secret. My beautiful magic hair can be styled! Yes it can, in any length, long or short, here's how: For long hair gently pull my hidden ponytail to its full length and lock it into the hidden slot. Now you are ready to comb my hair into many different styles. For short hair gently lift my ponytail out of the hidden slot and it will automatically return to a short length. Now you are ready to try some more styles using shorter hair. We are now ready to play, but remember, you must be gentle. Love, Dana." Uneeda stressed the word gentle in the instructions as the grow hair strand is easily pulled out of the head if pulled too hard. Dana is marked "©U.D.CO.INC./MCMLXX/MADE IN HONG KONG" on her head, and "©/U.D.CO.INC./MCMLXX/MADE IN HONG KONG/PAT.PEND." on her back. Her box is dated 1970. MIB (missing cello): **$20.00 – 25.00.** Loose: **$5.00 – 10.00.**

Kim: Kim is basically the same doll as Dana only with a different hair style and outfit. Her box is styled differently and doesn't have the side flaps as Dana's does. Kim's box is dated 1970 in Roman numerals and has the same message on the back as Dana's, only it reads "Love, Kim" at the end. NRFB: **$25.00 – 35.00.** Loose: **$5.00 – 10.00.**

Thum-Things: Turn the head on these dolls to change their expressions. Their boxes read "I'M THMART," "I'M THILLY," "I'M THLEEPY." The boxes are dated MCMXXIII (1973). The dolls were made in British Crown Colony of Hong Kong. MIB: **$15.00 – 20.00.** *Courtesy Robin Englehart, vintagelane.com, photo by Nancy Jean Mong.*

Grannykins: These 6" granny dolls came in several different outfits. Their boxes are dated 1974, and read "Made in the British Crown Colony of Hong Kong." The dolls are marked "©U.D. CO. INC./MCMLXXIV/MADE IN HONG KONG" on their heads and back. The dolls' glasses are painted on. MIB: **$15.00 – 20.00.**

Granny and Me and Grannykins: 16" doll with painted-on square granny glasses is shown next to the 6" Grannykins doll. Granny and Me originally came with a 7" granddaughter doll. The head mold used for Granny was also used on a number of other Uneeda dolls. The 16" doll is marked "UNEEDA DOLL/CO. INC./©1963" on her head. **$18.00 – 22.00.**

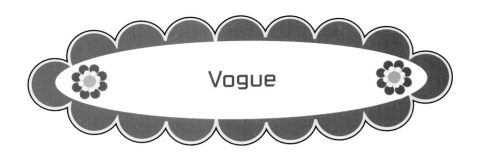

Too Dear: 23" doll designed by illustrator Eloise Wilkins to represent a two-year-old version of her Baby Dear One doll. The doll is all vinyl. Too Dear is marked "©/1963/E.Wilkin/Vogue Dolls" on her head. The doll in the photograph is wearing her original dress and shoes. **$175.00 – 225.00.**

Love Me Linda: This doll was released under two different names, Love Me Linda and Pretty as a Picture. The Love Me Linda in the photo is shown with her original box. The side of her box indicates that she was from the Ginny doll family. MIB: **$75.00 – 95.00.** *Courtesy Jennie Brott.*

Love Me Linda/Pretty as a Picture: In 1965 Sears sold these dolls under the name Love Me Linda. In 1965 the doll was shown in the J.C. Penney Christmas catalog and was listed simply as Toddler Doll. From 1967 to 1969 Montgomery Wards sold the doll under the name Pretty as a Picture. Pretty as a Picture came with a framed portrait of the doll. The Love Me Linda/Pretty as a Picture dolls are 15" tall and are marked "Vogue Doll ©1965." Some of these dolls have a tear drop molded in the vinyl under one of their eyes and other versions came without the tear drop. Some dolls are made of a nice quality, heavy vinyl that is lighter in color, while other dolls are made with a darker, more lightweight and brittle type of vinyl. The dolls in the photo are all wearing their original dresses with replaced shoes. Loose doll: **$25.00 – 40.00 each.** *Courtesy Jennie Brott.*

Pretty as a picture

Comes with her own framed portrait to hang on your wall!

$6 15 in.

This little girl has much, much more than her fair share of charm! You'll fall in love with her winsome brown eyes and delicate features. Her long golden hair is rooted, can be braided, brushed and cared for. She's 15 in. tall, enchanting in her Early American calico cotton dress and bloomers, long stockings, suede shoes. Stands alone, with jointed arms and legs. Portrait included. Ship. wt. 1 lb. 3 oz.
48 HT 10238—Doll and portrait..................6.00

3
Lisa and clothes
6⁹⁹ 18 in.

4
4⁹⁹ 12 in.
Doll and outfits

Toddlers

Two special dolls for a Christmas to remember!

1,2 Meet our lovely Debutante and Crown Princess—truly treasures to be kept for years. If a little loving leaves a fingerprint behind, just treat their complexions to a bit of soap and water. Their luxurious hair is gossamer soft, yet firmly rooted and washable. Both stand alone, have fully jointed vinyl bodies that only look fragile. They have angelic moving eyes with extra-long lashes, even tiny fingernails with pale pink polish. Beautiful story-book costumes are removable. Masterpieces from Italy, 14½ in. tall.

(1) Darling Debutante wears her cascade of shining hair braided with daisies. She comes in dainty eyelet dress, gloves, panties, stockings and slippers.
48 HT 10295—Ship. wt. 1 lb. 8 oz.............10.00

(2) Crown Princess carries an organdy parasol to complement her fully-lined velvet gown. Real feathers trim her bonnet, accent her shimmering curls. Wears ruffled organdy petticoat and pantaloons, hoopskirt, stockings and dancing slippers.
48 HT 10294—Ship. wt. 2 lbs. 6 oz............15.00

Pretty Lisa can stand by herself!

3 All three of Lisa's pretty dresses show off her lovely coloring. She has thick, lustrous rooted hair, is 18 in. tall, jointed, with big blue moving eyes.
48 HT 10239—Ship. wt. 2 lbs. 15 oz.............6.99

Sweetums comes with lots of clothes

4 Sweetums has a whole play-party-bedtime wardrobe, plus accessories to style her curly rooted hair. She's 12 in. tall, jointed, and can stand by herself.
48 HT 10240—Ship. wt. 1 lb. 7 oz.............4.99

1 Debutante
$10 14½ in.

2 Princess
$15 14½ in.

214 WARDS ALL

Pretty as a Picture: Montgomery Wards 1967 Christmas catalog showing Pretty as a Picture and her framed portrait. MIB doll with portrait: **$75.00 – 95.00.**

Toddler dolls

"Pretty as a Picture" $6 15 in.

Comes with her own framed portrait to hang on your wall 'cause she's so pretty!

1 This winsome lass has large brown eyes and long rooted hair that you can brush and comb. She's 15 inches tall and so enchanting in her lace-edged calico dress complete with cameo, stretch panty hose, and suede shoes. She will stand alone or sit because she's fully jointed. Portrait incl.
48 T 10237—Ship. wt. 1 lb. 8 oz.......Doll and portrait 6.00

Sweet Miss and wardrobe 4.99 16 in.

2 Pretty 16-inch sweetheart can stand alone, open and close her lovely brown eyes, is fully jointed. Her long rooted hair is fun to style new ways. She's ready for a party in her lace-trimmed dress, panties, shoes and stockings. Her 4-piece wardrobe includes 2 dresses, slacks and blouse—all with snap closures to make dressing her easy.
48 T 10293—Ship. wt. 1 lb. 12 oz..........Complete 4.99

Pretty as a Picture: Montgomery Wards 1968 Christmas catalog shows a differently dressed Pretty as a Picture doll. MIB doll with portrait: **$75.00 – 95.00.**

"Pretty as a Picture"

Comes with her own framed portrait to hang on your wall!

7.99 15 in.

She's charming—a winsome lass with huge brown eyes and delicate features. Her pretty, waist-length hair can be combed, brushed, braided or set as you choose. Fully jointed body, can stand alone or sit. Quaint calico print dress with petticoat has a deep flounce and puff sleeves of nylon, edged in lace. Velvet bodice. Wears panties, long stockings and suede slippers. Portrait about 6 by 7 in. is included—to hang on wall or stand on dresser. Ship. wt. 1 lb. 13 oz.
48 T 10266.............7.99

Pretty as a Picture: Montgomery Wards 1969 Christmas catalog shows still another version of Pretty as a Picture doll. MIB doll with portrait: **$75.00 – 95.00.**

Whitman

PeePul Pals: Whitman Publishing, primarily known for children's books, paper dolls, coloring books, and other paper products issued a line of nine storybook dolls called PeePul Pals. Each Peepul Pal doll came packaged inside a plastic house-shaped case with a storybook and several small accessories to act out the story line. The Peepul Pals included Cinderella, Little Red Riding Hood, Goldilocks, Rock-A-Bye Baby, Mother Goose, Betty Ballerina, Nina Nurse, Brenda Bride, and Sally Stewardess. The PeePul Pals are ½" tall and their tags read "Peepul Pal Doll by Whitman, Japan." Shown in the photo is Goldilocks. Mint in original case with accessories: **$30.00 – 45.00.**
Courtesy Robin Englehart, vintagelane.com, photo by Nancy Jean Mong.

PeePul Pals: Inside of Goldilock's case showing her story book and accessories.
Courtesy Robin Englehart, vintagelane.com, photo by Nancy Jean Mong.

PeePul Pals: Betty PeePul Pal inside her original plastic case. Mint in original case with accessories: **$30.00 – 45.00.** *Courtesy Robin Englehart, vintagelane.com, photo by Nancy Jean Mong.*

PeePul Pals: Inside of Betty Ballerina's case showing her story book and accessories. *Courtesy Robin Englehart, vintagelane.com, photo by Nancy Jean Mong.*

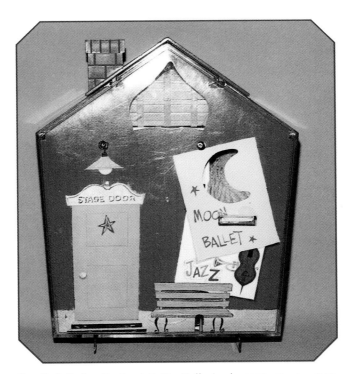

PeePul Pals: Back of Betty Ballerina's case. *Courtesy Robin Englehart, vintagelane.com, photo by Nancy Jean Mong.*

231

by Cindy Sabulis

It was December 1969 and television was bombarding young girls with advertisements for a wonderful new ballerina doll by Mattel. The doll was Dancerina, a 24" vinyl goddess, dressed head to toe in shocking ballerina pink. A translucent pink plastic crown was welded to the top of Dancerina's head. On her pointed toes she wore removable plastic ballet slippers and when she stood on the tips of those pink-covered toes, Danceria could do pirouettes with perfection. Although batteries were the thing that made Dancerina come to life, her mechanical crown was where the real magic lay. When the knob inside the crown was pushed down or pulled up, this doll danced like no doll before her had ever danced. Dancerina was truly the prima donna of the doll world.

It didn't take too many commercials to convince me Dancerina was the doll I just had to have for Christmas that year. Unfortunately, my sister Patty who was two years older than me and my sister Amy who was three years younger than me were seeing the same television commercials I was and they also just had to have this doll. With all three of us clamoring choruses of "I want Dancerina!" in our parents' ears, it was almost certain that out of fairness, none of us would get her.

Perhaps it was because a ballerina doll was something my sisters and I could identify with that we all wanted her. Each of us was at the time taking ballet lessons and had been almost from the time we started walking. At one time or another, each of us had worn a ballerina costume similar to Dancerina's and even imagined we could dance as well as the mechanical doll could. Whether it was because we could identify with her, or whether it was because a battery-operated dancing doll was the hottest thing going at the time, the three of us wanted this doll a great deal. I wanted Dancerina more than I remember wanting any other doll. To this day, I am convinced that I wanted her much more than my two sisters did. Of course, I'm sure if you ask them, they will tell you differently.

A couple of weeks before Christmas arrived I snuck a peek inside some storage eaves in an upstairs corner of our house. There is a slim chance I may have been snooping for Christmas presents. I'm sure if you ask my sisters, they'll tell you I was, but I don't think that is why I happened to peek into the darkest corner of those eaves. For whatever reason possessed me to look there, when I searched inside the eaves, there right smack in front of me was Dancerina's happy face smiling at me from the front of her box. Of course, I didn't see her until after I removed a mountain of junk that was originally obstructing the view of her box. Quickly covering the doll up, I ran away from the eaves thrilled with my find. For a short time I walked around glowing in the knowledge that I was getting Dancerina for Christmas. But slowly another not-so-pleasant thought crept into my mind. What if it wasn't me who got her? What if that wonderful doll was unwrapped by one of my sisters? What if Dancerina ended up in their arms Christmas morning instead of my own? Finally, unable to keep my find to myself, I spilled the beans to one of my older long-past-the-doll-wanting-age sisters that I had "accidentally" discovered Dancerina hidden behind a pile of stuff in the storage eaves. My older and wiser sister curtly informed me that the doll was not for any of us, but instead was a gift for a child of one of my mother's friend's. Our mother was holding it for her friend because the friend had no place to hide presents in her house. It sounded fishy even to my young mind, but it did cast some doubt as to whether this doll would really be under our tree that year.

Christmas morning finally came and was filled with lots of excitement and noise as my siblings and I anxiously tore open gift after gift. Somewhere among the chaos of opening presents, a gift was passed out and the tag read, "To Patty, Cindy, and Amy." I immediately recognized the size of the gift as being the same as Dancerina's box which I had seen in the eaves. My two sisters and I awkwardly unwrapped the present together. Sure enough, there she was. The doll we all *had* to have — Dancerina. But a doll to share? How in the world do you share a doll with two sisters? Dolls were meant to have one mother only, not two and certainly not three. Being close in ages, naturally my sisters and I had shared a lot over the years. There were times we had to share a bedroom, times we had to share clothing, we sometimes shared the same friends, and often had to share toys. But never before had I ever had to share in the ownership of a doll with my sisters. It just couldn't work, could it? Which young mother would get to play with Dancerina first? Which lucky girl would get to operate her for her first dance recital? Which sister would that beautiful doll get to sleep with at the end of the day?

I honestly don't remember how my sisters and I worked out the logistics of owning a doll together. If we ever fought over her, I have long ago forgotten about it. When I started to collect dolls not too long after I stopped playing with them Patty and Amy willingly let me add Dancerina to my doll collection. They had no interest in her any longer — or any doll for that matter. Sadly, Dancerina's dancing days are over. A combination of battery corrosion and loose wires has played havoc with the doll's mechanical insides. Her plastic crown is broken in several places, her hair is a mess, and her poor arms after being unsuccessfully glued on many times over the years are now held on with masking tape. Her once rosy lips and bright cheeks have dulled with age and she bears little resemblance to the sparkling face that beamed at me from under the eaves more than three decades ago.

Even in the pitiful state our Dancerina doll is in, she still holds a special place of honor among my collection of dolls. Her condition shows how well-loved she was, not just by one, but by three girls many years ago.

The author's and her sisters' childhood Dancerina doll.

About the Author

Cindy Sabulis is involved in many aspects of doll collecting. She and her husband Steve are owners of Toys of Another Time, a business specializing in dolls from the 1950s through the 1970s. Together they sell at doll shows and from their website at www.dollsntoys.com. Cindy has written dozens of articles about collecting for doll and collectible publications. She is the co-author of *The Collector's Guide to Tammy,* the Ideal Teen and the author of the first volume of *Dolls of the 1960s and 1970s.* She is an advisor/contributor for *Schroeder's Collectible Toys, Garage Sale & Flea Market Annual,* and *Flea Market Trader* providing information and values on Tammy, Liddle Kiddles, Tressy, Littlechaps, and many other dolls and their accessories. During her college years, Cindy worked for numerous regional and national publications as a freelance writer and editor. After she earned her BS in computer science she went to work full time in the computer field, but continued to write in her spare time. In 1990 she started up her business selling dolls part time out of her home. A year later she left the corporate world to devote more time to writing and expanding her business. Her husband joined her full time in the business several years later. Steve and Cindy have a 12 year old son, David.

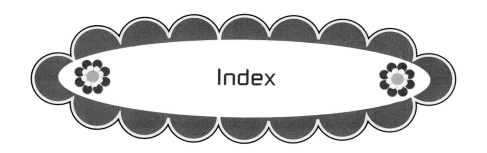

Index

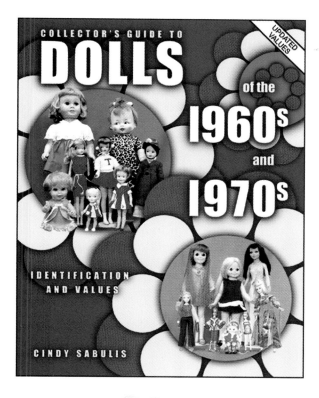

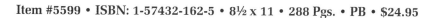